HELPING KIDS COPE

A PARENTS GUIDE TO STRESS MANAGEMENT

DR. ARNOLD BURRON

Accent Books™ is an imprint of David C. Cook Publishing Co.
David C. Cook Publishing Co., Elgin, Illinois 60120
David C. Cook Publishing Co., Weston, Ontario
Nova Distribution Ltd., Newton Abbot, England

HELPING KIDS COPE
©1988 by Arnold Burron
(Original title: *Children and Stress*)

Cover design by Graphically Speaking, Inc.
First Printing, 1988
Printed in the United States of America
96 95 94 93 92 7 6 5 4 3
Library of Congress Catalog Card Number 87-71220
ISBN 0-78140-476-2

To
Darold, Charah, Keith, and Cathy
"Arrows"

Contents

A Note to Parents

Childhood stress and its negative effects upon young people of all ages are documented facts. Even the public schools, in a well-meaning but misguided attempt to respond to the problem of stress in children, have introduced procedures to teach children visualization techniques, relaxation exercises, and other activities to reduce stress. Psychologists have been consulted for their theories about reducing stress in children. Research has been conducted to identify causes, effects, and responses to stress in children. Educators have been polled for their considered opinions about how to reduce stress in children. In short, no stone has been left unturned in searching the vast fields of contemporary knowledge for solutions to the serious problem of children and stress.

What has been missing in this diligent search, however, is a study of wisdom. Wisdom, not knowledge, holds the only real solution to lasting and effective methods of helping children build the strength of character necessary to confront and manage, not only day-to-day stresses of childhood, but catastrophic stress that can literally destroy lives. For the purposes of our discussion, we have defined "children" as those under the age of eighteen; the legal age of personal accountability.

This book about stress and children is different from any other book on this topic. It is different because it looks first to the wisdom of Scripture for answers to the problem of stress and children. Contemporary knowledge is not overlooked, but it is considered in its proper perspective. Thousands of years of insight, derived from God's Word, constitute the foundation of this book. Wisdom about what to teach children, about how to teach them, and about the dynamic results of scripturally-guided teaching is offered in sharp contrast to contemporary knowledge and modern theory which proliferate in secular approaches to children and stress.

CHAPTER ONE

Facts Christian Parents *Must* Know

Have you ever done anything outstandingly courageous in the face of an emergency? something so brave that you surprised even yourself? something that you could refer to later with the words, "I didn't know I had it in me!"?

If you've ever had the privilege of being brave—of "being there" when you were needed—you enjoy a rare experience. Most of us can only wonder how we would react in a situation of emergency, where mere seconds mean the difference between triumph and tragedy.

Not only do most of us wonder how we might react, but many of us, down deep, harbor a secret fear that we might not react nobly at all and that cowardice or uncertainty would hold sway over courage and action. The thought that we might fail to act when needed is not unfounded. There is even a term for it in psychology. It is called "Bystander Apathy." It is what happened in 1962 when, in a first case of its kind to be reported in the media, almost forty people over a period of forty-five minutes inexplicably failed to do anything to help Kitty Genovese as she was repeatedly assaulted and brutally murdered on a street in New York City, right outside the windows of the passive observers.

Numerous other cases of Bystander Apathy have been

reported in the media:

> A man was beaten and stabbed to death in New York's Central Park. Not one of the thirty people who saw what happened came to his aid.
>
> A young woman fled, in broad daylight, down the median of a busy divided highway, frantically beckoning for help in escaping a belligerent male pursuer. Not one of the occupants of scores of automobiles passing by stopped to come to her aid.
>
> One researcher, exploring the problem of "Bystander Apathy," reported that in 20 replications of a staged "crisis" situation, no witnesses to the crisis attempted to intervene or to call the police. In another staged situation simulating a theft which took place with a uniformed and armed policeman nearby, *no* witness bothered to inform the policeman.[1]

No Christian would want to think that he or she would be a victim of Bystander Apathy. First John 3:16-18 tells us:

> We know love by this, that He laid down His life for us; and we ought to lay down our lives for the brethren. But whoever has the world's goods, and beholds his brother in need and closes his heart against him, how does the love of God abide in Him? Little children, let us not love with word or with tongue, but in deed and truth.

While this deals specifically with relationships between believers, the parable of the Good Samaritan (Luke 10:30-37) commands our involvement with anyone in need. If some specialized training were readily available, most of us would be eager to do whatever it takes and to learn whatever is necessary in order to be able to predict with confidence that we would act with undaunted courage in an emergency where only the best and the most brave could meet the challenge.

It is encouraging to realize that specialized training, based on Biblical principles is available. Every day as a parent, you face these same, sometimes overwhelming, situations. Every day you face the awesome responsibility of shaping your child's life: attitudes, values, morals, spiritual commitment.

Your courage in assuming your role as a parent may never make the Six-o'-clock News, but it is nonetheless real. It must encompass not only taking appropriate actions when necessary, but also being a preventive bulwark against tragedy, alienation, and fear.

Closely related to the concern about Bystander Apathy is the concern of every human being about how he or she would react in the face of personal tragedy. It's not uncommon to hear people say, "I'd go to pieces, . . ." or "I wouldn't be able to take it, . . ." or "I'd rather die than . . ." or similar expressions of how people anticipate they would react in the face of adversity or tragedy.

We profess our faith in a good and gracious God, but we wonder how we would react if the policeman at the door bore the dreaded news that our child or spouse had been killed in an accident. How would we respond if the doctor told us that our stubborn ailment gave us a prognosis of only six more months to live? or that we would be permanently disfigured? And what gnaws with equal ferocity at the heart of a parent is the question of how our child would react in the face of tragedy—if our child had to face death. Or disfigurement. Or the loss of a sibling, or another loved one, or of his parents. How would bitter animosity and exclusion by a peer group affect him, or loneliness and despair? How will our children face adversity and tragedy?

These concerns are what this book is all about. But as serious as the subject matter is, and as unpleasant and difficult as it is to talk about some of the stresses our children face, this is not a book about tragedy. It is a book about triumph—about how to build stress-triumphant children who can face and overcome adversity.

In the explanation of Bystander Apathy, there was a partial note of encouragement for us because there is the *possibility*, through appropriate training, of producing people who will probably act with courage in an emergency.[2] When we talk about how our children will react to adversity and tragedy, though, there is *absolute* encouragement. There is not just the possibility of producing people who will probably manage with courage the stress of adversity and tragedy; there is absolute certainty that our children will positively manage with courage and forbearance the stress of adversity and tragedy. How? Before we expand upon this, let's look at some facts about children and stress.

Fact 1: There are two types of stress your child can face—positive stress (or, as professionals call it, "eustress") and negative stress. Either type of stress can lead to distress and to a host of negative results. In other words, too much success is not good and too many problems aren't good.

Fact 2: How your child reacts to stress is more important than the type of stress he faces or how much stress he faces.

Fact 3: All children will face negative stress. Negative stress is unqualifiedly predicted—promised—in the Bible. John 16:33 assures us, "These things I have spoken to you, that in Me you may have peace. In the world you have tribulation, but take courage; I have overcome the world." It is part of being a human being. Your child will face one or more of the following: illness, accident, failure, tragedy, persecution, loneliness, rejection, injustice, poverty, hardship, disillusionment.

Fact 4: There are two ways to deal with negative stress.

1. Stress avoidance.
2. Stress management.

Stress avoidance means that certain decisions, behaviors, and actions can keep one from ever having to face situations of extreme difficulty. But to practice stress avoidance, a child must possess qualities of wisdom, insight, prudence, maturity, and discretion—qualities so rare in children as to be virtually nonexistent.

Stress management is the second way to deal with negative stress. Since some stresses, such as illness, failure, and others listed above are not avoidable, they must be managed. To manage stress, people need inner resources, hardiness, and strength of character[3] as well as confidence, faith, and a positive outlook. Again, these qualities are so rare in children that the child who possesses them is immediately recognized as an exceptional child.

Fact 5: Although the qualities needed for stress avoidance are rare in children, some do possess them. What is more important, these qualities are available to every child. They can be taught by every parent. The content and the methods are given in the Bible. They have been successfully used for thousands of years, and they are yours to use today.

Fact 6: Although the qualities needed for stress management are rarely found in children, these qualities, too, can be taught, or rather, instilled. Inner resources of strength, hardiness, character, confidence, faith, and a positive outlook are available to every child. They can be taught by every parent. What to teach and how to teach them are presented in the Bible, and outlined in this book.

Fact 7: Helping children manage stress from a Christian

perspective produces behaviors in children which are totally different than the behaviors sought by secular child-development specialists or child psychologists. Secular specialists seek to produce children who are *well-adjusted* to the values and behaviors of contemporary society. Christian counselors seek to produce children who are *maladjusted* to the values and behaviors of today's society. The Christian is forewarned by Jesus Christ that society—the world—will reject him; there is a social price to pay for following a Christian value system. Second Timothy 3:12 promises, "And indeed, all who desire to live godly in Christ Jesus will be persecuted." First John 3:13 warns, "Do not marvel, brethren, if the world hates you."

More about this later, but the fact is worth restating: Secular counsel on helping children manage stress *may be totally inappropriate* for Christian parents. Wisdom and spiritual discernment are necessary. Secular books, magazines, pamphlets, or classes which teach parents how to help children manage stress may contain useful suggestions. They may also contain very harmful suggestions for Christian children.

In one book written from a foundation of secular philosophy, the authors discuss the topic of death. Their advice on what to tell children about heaven and about loved ones who have "gone to heaven" leaves no doubt about where they stand:

What serves us best in our efforts to help children deal with death and dying is the truth. What confuses children the most are evasions, myths, half-truths, fables, and lies which are meant to comfort, but ultimately create more fear.[4]

Heaven, life everlasting, and our hope in Christ are, in their definition, "lies!"

Contrast this advice with the words of the Apostle Paul. He wrote to the Christians at Thessalonica to comfort them and ease their sorrow at the deaths of their friends:

But we do not want you to be uninformed, brethren, about those who are asleep, that you may not grieve, as do the rest who have no hope. For if we believe that Jesus died and rose again, even so God will bring with Him those who have fallen asleep in Jesus. (I Thessalonians 4:13-14)

The victory of Christ's return and the resurrection fill the rest of I Thessalonians 4. It is this victory and hope that secular "authorities" criticize as being harmful!

It is an absolutely indisputable fact that all advice on children and stress which does not derive directly from God's Word must be measured against the Scriptures.

Christian parents *must be aware* of the underlying philosophies of secular authorities and measure *all* advice against the clear teaching and reality of the Bible. If the advice contradicts God's Word, don't take it!

Fact 8: The Bible identifies one major goal for parents in raising their children. This goal directly affects and determines what we teach our children to help them manage stress and *how* we teach them. *The primary, paramount, most important and immeasurably significant goal of any parent, to be sought regardless of the price—including the subordination of all other goals—worth any sacrifice, including your life, is your child's eternal salvation.*

The following excerpt, taken from the book, *Discipline That Can't Fail,* explains this goal.

> The patriarch Abraham recognized this fact as an indisputable truth. His recognition was evidenced in his willing and unhesitating obedience to God, even if it meant his son Isaac had to die.
>
> This same truth is taught over and over again in the Scriptures. Jesus said, "For what does it profit a man to gain the whole world, and

forfeit his soul?" (Mark 8:36). Jesus also told His disciples, "Lay up for yourselves treasures in heaven, where neither moth nor rust destroys, and where thieves do not break in or steal; for where your treasure is, there will your heart be also." (Matthew 6:20-21).

The Apostle Paul emphatically directed the Colossians to get their values straightened out. "Set your mind on the things above," he declared, "not on the things that are on earth. For you have died and your life is hidden with Christ in God." (Colossians 3:2-3).

Peter, also writing to Jewish Christians who lived in an empire sated with materialistic pleasures, anxiously exhorted them, "Beloved, I urge you as aliens and strangers to abstain . . ." from the things that would wage war against their souls. (I Peter 2:11).

There is absolutely no question—no room for debate of any kind—that the whole message of God's Word focuses on the fact that salvation is the most important goal a parent can have for his child.[5]

It follows, then, by the rules of logic, that any techniques, methods, procedures, approaches, or principles we teach our children to help them manage stress should contribute to our major goal for them as Christian parents.

Questions for Parents

1. What kinds of stress do you see your children experiencing now?
   Be specific.

2. Are these stresses positive or negative?

3. How do your children react to stress? Give specific symptoms characteristic to each individual child.

Child 1:   (name)

Child 2:   (name)

Child 3:   (name)

4. How have you helped your child avoid stress?

5. How have you helped your child manage stress?

Questions for Children and Parents

Children often see situations much differently than adults. If your child is old enough, discuss these questions and the answers with him/her.

1. What kinds of things bother you? (You may need to give examples.)

2. What kinds of problems do you have? Do any of the kids want to fight with you? Does anyone make fun of you? What for?

3. How do you feel when things like this happen?

4. Mom and/or Dad want to help. Sometimes we do not know the right questions to ask, and we may

not know the right thing to do. But let's talk about the problems and ways to resolve them.

5. Make this a specific prayer request. Write down the problem(s); look up Scripture verses relating to it, and pray specifically for God's help.

Problem/Stress Scripture Prayer Request

[1] Jerry Bergman, "The Sociology of Bystander Apathy," *Journal of the American Scientific Affiliation,* Volume 37: No. 1, March, 1985, pp. 31-32.

[2] See note 1.

[3] Arnold H. Burron, and Jerry Crews, *Guaranteed Steps to Managing Stress* (Wheaton, Illinois: Tyndale House Publishers, 1986), p. 204.

[4] Donald Medeiros, et al., *Children Under Stress: How to Help With the Every-Day Stresses of Childhood.* (Englewood Cliffs: Prentice-Hall, Inc., 1983), p. 183.

[5] Arnold H. Burron, *Discipline That Can't Fail* (Grand Rapids, Michigan: Mott Media & Baker Book House, 1984), pp. 8-9.

CHAPTER TWO

Your Child's First Line of Defense Against Stress

CARINA O'HAYRE IS a young mother who has what it takes as a stress manager. Carina did something out of the ordinary when she decided not to send her son Ryan to kindergarten on the first day of school. Ryan was one of those "borderline" cases. He was just old enough to make the cut-off date for acceptance into school. He could be sent to school, or he could be held back for a year at his parents' discretion and still comply with the compulsory attendance laws of the state where his parents lived. Ryan was intelligent, articulate, curious, and active. His attention span was normal for children of his age, and he enjoyed learning. In short, he possessed all of what professional educators call "readiness factors" for entrance into school.

Ryan would also be almost a full year younger than a number of his classmates, guaranteeing that, barring misfortune or illness, he would probably graduate from high school and college as the youngest person in his class. He would have a head start in the job market and in beginning his climb up whatever corporate or professional ladder he would choose.

But Carina was not an ordinary parent. Carina resisted the pressure of well-meaning friends, goal-oriented relatives, and, yes, even Ryan's grandparents, who were the very embodiment of the American Work Ethic, and instead sought professional input from a variety of sources. She talked to her pediatrician. She consulted with me, since I had been one of her college instructors. She visited the kindergarten Ryan was scheduled to attend, and she spent time in prayer. Ultimately, Carina decided that more negative stress than positive stress was possible if Ryan entered school as an early pupil. Carina looked ahead. She anticipated that Ryan would probably do very well academically, but that it was both possible and probable that certain avoidable negative stresses would be imposed upon Ryan in the future:

1. The stress of being physically less developed than his classmates, which might pose a problem in certain activities requiring physical maturity.

2. The stress of, perhaps, being emotionally less mature than his classmates during the critical years of puberty.

3. The stress of possibly being socially less mature, and of being rejected by an older peer group at any stage of his formal education.

4. The stress of possibly being "the youngest" in all of his formal and informal relationships such as Sunday school, youth group excursions, and similar activities which might mean being excluded (by being under the legal age) from activities such as amusement park rides, driving, and so forth.

One other concern Carina had was that Ryan might be bored when he did enter school a year later. Her professional advisors, however, assured her that the possible stress of boredom was not likely; good schools individualize academic programs to accommodate differences. Weighed objectively, the most probable stress for Ryan would occur if he entered school as an early pupil.

Carina made a decision which will have profound implications for Ryan. Rather than expose Ryan to unnecessary stress which she would have to help him *manage,* she made a decision to avoid the stress altogether. It took courage for Carina to confront the "success" ethic. It took courage for her to undergo the personal stress of subtle and overt pressures to pay obeisance to the sacred cow of academic achievement, "giftedness" in her child, and the "get-to-the-top-as-soon-as-you-can-as-fast-as-you-can" prevailing values. Carina experienced a level of discomfort, and holding Ryan out of school will constitute an inconvenience for her, but her discomfort and inconvenience were a small price to pay. She was her child's first line of defense against negative stress that posed the probability of being harmful to him.

Had Carina felt Ryan was ready, she would have acted on that knowledge and enrolled him. The point is, Carina knew her child. You can, too.

YOU ARE YOUR CHILD'S FIRST LINE OF DEFENSE

Carina performed an important function required of all parents. She protected her child. Unfortunately, many parents do not realize that this protective function extends beyond the physical level. The Bible clearly defines a parent's role as a protector, to include protecting children against emotional and spiritual harm (Proverbs 2: Ephesians 6:4; Colossians 3:21). The Bible is also clear that we are to achieve this goal by persuasion, teaching, or by compulsion—force. (See Proverbs 2:1-3; 5-15; 3:1-4; 13:24; 29:15.)

Notice that we are talking here about harmful stress. Not all difficulties are harmful. At the end of this chapter, in the section entitled "How Do I Know When to Intervene?", some guidelines are provided on how to decide when to step in.

But now, let's take a look at your second task as a parent. When harmful stress can't be avoided, you may have to intervene and manage the stressful situation for your child.

Perhaps your child is in a situation where he needs help. He is not managing the harmful stress very well. You need to step in, whether or not he wants you to do so.

HELPING YOUR CHILD MANAGE HARMFUL STRESS

There are a number of reasons why you must step in even if your child doesn't want you to do so.

1. You are directly responsible for your child's well-being. This responsibility is uniquely yours and is recognized not only by the civil courts but also by the Bible.

2. You are in a much better position to evaluate possible sources of stress for your child than your child is because you have the advantage of maturity and experience.

3. Oftentimes a source of stress renders your child powerless. He does not have the authority to change a stressful situation, nor does he have the persuasive powers or abilities to change attitudes or behaviors in others who might be the source of his stress.

4. When a person is under stress, she is often so occupied with coping with the stress itself that she is unable to analyze the source of the stress in a detached, calm, and critical manner. When your child is under stress you can perform this function for her.

5. Even if your child is able to recognize a source of stress, he may, because of his limited experience, see very few alternatives for dealing with it. You, on the other hand, may see many more avenues to help your child totally avoid stress or manage it.

A parent has scriptural as well as legal authority and responsibility for the well-being of his child. A parent is also the best-equipped person to help his child deal with stress. An observant parent will be the first person to notice signs of stress or distress in his child, and if communication has been established at an early age, the parent is in a position to initiate action to help the child cope with stress.

Even though the conclusions above are logical, defensible, and inescapable, it is not always easy to act as your child's first line of defense against stress. Ironically, your own fears of rejection, embarrassment, or inadequacy may prevent effective action. Consider the following situation, which is a stress-filled situation for a number of people but, in particular, for a sixteen-year-old student.

> Communication in the Grayson household had always been excellent. Almost unconsciously, however, Becky Grayson's mother began to notice subtle changes in Becky's behavior. Not that Becky had become outright rude or difficult. She wasn't that type of child. She was always courteous, respectful, and helpful around the house. But there were gradual changes in her behavior which could be described as "mild." Nevertheless, some instinctive reaction on Mrs. Grayson's part caused her to take notice. Becky had begun to get tired very early in the evening and to go to bed earlier than usual. She seemed slower to laugh along with family jokes and to participate in family fun. At the dinner table, the usually chatty and conversational Becky, while not sullen, was quiet and polite, certainly not her usual, ebullient self. She would come home from school and from volleyball practice and do an almost convincing job of enthusiastically declaring how much fun she was having at practice. But her increasing fatigue, quietness, and seeming aloofness told her parents that something was not right. What

wasn't right became obvious the first time
the parents attended a school volleyball
game.

Junior varsity competition took place in sets
of three games. Becky's team had no problem at all defeating the opposition school in
the first game. But Becky didn't get to play.
In the second game, another lopsided victory
seemed sure to occur. Most of Becky's
teammates were rotated in and out of the
game frequently, except for Becky and two of
her friends who sat quietly on the end of the
bench, hoping desperately to be noticed by
the coach. But the coach seemed to be
oblivious to their presence. During time-
outs, the girls would feign a fighting spirit
and a cheerful attitude and gather with the
rest of the team in the huddle, yelling their
encouragement and enthusiasm, but the
coach did not seem to notice. Finally, when
the score stood at 13 to 2, with victory
assured, Becky's parents began to get fidgety.
Certainly now the coach would notice the
three girls sitting at the end of the bench,
hoping feverishly that their chances of getting
into the game would be enhanced by the
lopsided score. But for some inexplicable
reason, the coach kept in the starting line-up
and soundly trounced the other team. Two
games out of three declared the contest to be
over. As the teams left the court, Mr.
Grayson observed one of the "bench sitters"
gallantly choking back tears as she trailed
behind her teammates into the locker room.

On the way home from the game, Mr. and Mrs. Grayson tactfully suggested to Becky that perhaps it would have been appropriate for her to be put into the game. Becky, however, in her own peculiar way of dealing with the stress of her disappointment and the violation of her own sense of fair play, staunchly defended the coach's actions. Repeating frequently that the coach was "a good coach," she declared that the coach had, perhaps, only unconsciously played favorites. But it was obvious to Mr. and Mrs. Grayson that even though the coach was a competent coach, and that the skill levels of the players were not all equal, the three players who had sat in eager expectation on the bench deserved to participate fully in a volleyball game which was a part of the school's extracurricular enrichment program.

The situation of little or no playing time, except for a select few, repeated itself over the course of the next several games. When Becky inexplicably broke into tears over a minor incident at home, Mr. and Mrs. Grayson knew that some action had to be taken. Their child was in a stressful situation. She felt rejected, and her self-confidence was being systematically attacked and destroyed. Even though Becky participated in practices and faithfully tried to carry out the coach's every instruction, she still got to play only rarely. And even though there was no outright rejection by the rest of the team, it was obvious that Becky and her two teammates were not really valued members. They were, in essence, rejects. They never got into the game unless the situation was either hopelessly lost or absolutely won. Obviously, their contribution was really not relevant to the outcome. And it was logical for them to perceive themselves as irrelevant.

Over Becky's objections—because as a concerned parent her father knew that he could not always heed his child's objections when attempting to help her deal with problems—Mr. Grayson decided to take action. But he had to solve several related problems of concern to him.

First, Mr. Grayson felt uncomfortable about going to the school and talking to the coach.

Second, he was uneasy about the fact that it would seem to the coach, or to anyone else, that he was over-protective—a parent who was putting far too much emphasis upon a junior-varsity sports incident at so low a level in the child's high school experience.

Third, he didn't want to be considered a "stage parent," one who is always seeking the starring role or more playing time for his child even when it might be obvious that the child's participation was already at an appropriate and equitable level.

He also knew that it was going to be a difficult subject to broach, since, no matter how he brought up the topic, the coach would perceive it as a demand that his child be played during games.

There were a number of factors which led to Mr. Grayson's discomfort with the whole situation, which had now become stress filled for him.

It is at this point that many parents fail in their obligation to their children because they, themselves, are unable to handle the stress of being their child's first line of defense. They can handle "normal" stress, but they have great difficulty in handling the embarrassment and possible rejection by an authority figure should they need to put themselves on the line for their child. Nevertheless, Mr. Grayson accepted his responsibility.

It is interesting to note that all participants in this situation were possible victims of the same type of stress.

Consider this: Becky was suffering from the stress of rejection, embarrassment and inadequacy. Mr. Grayson, in having to engage in a number of direct actions which made him feel uncomfortable, was uneasy with the thought of rejection or outright hostility on the part of the teacher, or from other parents who might perceive him as a stage parent. He also faced the possibility that his daughter's teammates might discover that he had attempted to help his daughter and that she might be rejected not only by the coach but, also, now overtly by the players for allowing her father to interfere. The coach, also, faced feelings of inadequacy and possible rejection by a parent whose dissatisfaction was a statement of his rejection of her judgment, her coaching ability, and her professional expertise.

Fortunately, Mr. Grayson recognized these elements in the situation. He also recognized the need to follow the carefully-delineated scriptural principles in Matthew 18 to deal with this problem, which was basically an interpersonal problem. It is important to note and remember that Biblical principles can often be used in secular situations. In addressing the problem, Mr. Grayson attempted to minimize the potential amount of rejection the teacher could feel.

Happily, because of Mr. Grayson's awareness and acceptance of his responsibility to minimize his child's stress and because of his knowledge of specific principles laid out in the Scriptures for dealing with interpersonal problems, the source of the stress for Becky was resolved. How did he do it?

First, Mr. Grayson went directly to the coach. Fortunately, this step was enough. Had it not worked, he would have taken one or two others with him. Also, he tempered his conversation by reflecting on James 3:13-18; Colossians 3:17, and Ephesians 4:29-32.

Becky had responsible and concerned parents who were willing to take assertive action on her behalf. Other suggestions on how a parent can determine when to intervene directly in the child's behalf are presented throughout this book.

AT WHAT AGE SHOULD CHILDREN "FIGHT THEIR OWN BATTLES"?

At what point are children "too old" to have parents intervene in their behalf? Consider the case of David Shannon, a United States Air Force Academy cadet. He was expelled from the Air Force Academy as a result of accusations that he had violated the Academy "Honor Code." Cadet Shannon insisted that he was innocent. In reviewing transcripts of the hearings, David's father alleged that basic precepts of justice and fairness had been violated.

The expulsion of twenty-two-year-old David was a traumatic experience for him. The bureaucracy was too big for David to fight, the levels of administration and the legal barriers erected against him too sophisticated and too complex for him to understand. So David's father stepped in. Paul Shannon left behind a successful business in New Jersey and moved to Colorado Springs, Colorado, to carry part of his son's burden. He became actively involved in asserting his son's case. He endured hostility. He put up with ridicule. He tolerated discomfort, and he fought against buck-passing, excessive delays, and negative publicity. He persevered in his son's behalf with amazing tenacity. He believed in his son. He believed—and continues to believe—that his son is innocent. He is fighting for his son's honorable reinstatement. Was his son—at age twenty-two—embarrassed that his father was "fighting his battle?" To an audience of thousands of people on a secular radio station talk show in Denver, Colorado, David Shannon expressed his appreciation for his father's love and concern, and expressed, in turn his own love and admiration for his father.

At what point are children "too old" to have parents intervene in their behalf? At any age at which they do not *need* help. Paul Shannon, a Christian parent who perceived that his son had suffered an injustice and that his son was not able to effectively manage the stress of this injustice alone, decided that his son needed help. David Shannon's unashamed expression of love and gratitude is a dynamic witness to the fact that there is no age limit to helping your children.

HOW TO HELP YOUR CHILD HANDLE STRESS

In the next chapter of this book, sources of childhood stress will be identified and discussed. Whatever the source of childhood stress, however, and whatever the symptoms of childhood stress, there are certain activities a parent can do to help his or her child cope with stress. Those activities include:

1. Helping your child develop a strong sense of self-worth and a strong measure of self-confidence so that he can effectively deal with the stress of rejection or failure.

2. Helping your child develop strength of character in situations in which she needs to cope with unavoidable adversity.

3. Helping your child avoid the stress of uncertainty when faced with a direct challenge to his values and his belief system.

4. Helping your child identify sources of stress she can avoid, and teaching her ways to avoid these sources of stress.

5. Minimizing sources of stress in parent/child relationships.

6. Intervening at school on your child's behalf.

7. Intervening in out-of-school situations on your child's behalf.

The main point of this chapter bears repeating:

You are your child's first line of defense against stress. You can help your child avoid harmful stress by keeping him out of it. You help your child manage stress by stepping into it with her. You carry out these functions whether your child likes it or not. You do what you have to do even if it is uncomfortable or stressful for you.

HOW TO DECIDE WHEN TO INTERVENE

Chapter one in this book listed several facts about stress. One of these facts, in particular, is important in deciding when to intervene.

Fact 8: The primary, paramount, most important, and immeasurably significant goal of any parent, regardless of the price—including the subordination of all other goals—worth any sacrifice, including your life, is your child's eternal salvation.

This fact is so vital in any program of helping children manage stress that it should be indisputable. Unless we are absolutely certain that this is indisputable, unarguable, irrefutable, nondebatable—or however else we may say that we totally believe it—we cannot do an effective job of helping our children manage stress. And the only way to prove the truth of this fact is to look at what the Bible says about this goal.

> Now this is the commandment, the statutes
> and the judgments which the Lord your God
> has commanded me to teach you, that you
> might do them in the land where you are
> going over to possess it, so that you and your
> son and your grandson might fear the Lord
> your God, to keep all His statutes and His
> commandments, which I command you, all
> the days of your life, and that your days may
> be prolonged. O Israel, you should listen and
> be careful to do it, that it may be well with
> you and that you may multiply greatly, just as

the Lord, the God of your fathers, has promised you, in a land flowing with milk and honey. Hear, O Israel! The Lord is our God, the Lord is one! And you shall love the Lord your God with all your heart and with all your soul and with all your might. And these words, which I am commanding you today, shall be on your heart; and you shall teach them diligently to your sons and shall talk of them when you sit in your house and when you walk by the way and when you lie down and when you rise up. . . . When your son ask you in time to come, saying, "What do the testimonies and the statutes and the judgments mean which the Lord commanded you?" then you shall say to your son, "We were slaves to Pharaoh in Egypt; and the Lord brought us from Egypt with a mighty hand. . . ." So the Lord commanded us to observe all these statutes, to fear the Lord our God for our good always and for our survival, as it is today. And it will be righteousness for us if we are careful to observe all this commandment before the Lord our God, just as He commanded us. (Deuteronomy 6:1-7, 20-21, 24-25)

Some logical conclusions have to follow if we believe our primary goal is to provide the guidance and the conditions necessary to build spiritual strength or faith.

Faith is built in three ways:
1. Through prayer.
2. Through Bible study.
3. Through adversity.

Adversity is nothing less than negative stress. Our decision, then, concerning when to intervene in a situation of negative stress depends upon the answer to this question:

Will this stress *strengthen* my child's *faith,* or will this stress be *spiritually damaging* to him?

Not all negative stress is bad for children. Children need to confront problems, analyze possible solutions, and make good decisions in solving problems. They need to be able to fight some of their own battles and withstand pressure. As parents, we need to be there to listen, to probe gently and question, to offer gentle guidance, and to encourage our children. We need to watch carefully and monitor their progress. But if we observe certain signs that tell us the stress is too heavy (see chapter three), or if we sense that our child's faith is being weakened rather than strengthened, we need to intervene.

It is likely that our child is growing in faith through a stressful situation when he or she shows these positive behaviors:

1. He is able to talk with us about his problem.

2. She is able to retain her composure when discussing the problem. That is, the discussion doesn't end with a flood of tears, an abrupt decision not to talk anymore, a raising of voices, or other signs of acute emotion.

3. He is able to discuss possible solutions with a trusted adult.

4. She is able to participate in prayer about the problem.

5. He is able to listen and carefully consider parental input from God's Word, pertinent Bible texts, or Scripture narratives that relate to the problem.

Consider this statement from Romans 5:3-5:

> Not only this, but we also exult in our
> tribulations, knowing that tribulation brings
> about perseverance; and perseverance, proven

character; and proven character, hope; and
hope does not disappoint, because the love of
God has been poured out within our hearts
through the Holy Spirit who was given to us.

Resist the urge to follow, in total, the advice of secular psychologists or child specialists. Many of their children are tragic examples of secular wisdom and the rejection of what God has outlined in His Word. Then, follow one more step in being your child's first line of defense against stress.

THE EXAMPLE OF JAMES

Hundreds of years ago, the Apostle James pointed the early Christians (and us!) to a tremendous source of power. He wrote, under the inspiration of the Holy Spirit, these words:

The effective prayer of a righteous man can
accomplish much. Elijah was a man with a
nature like ours, and he prayed earnestly that
it might not rain; and it did not rain on the
earth for three years and six months. And he
prayed again, and the sky poured rain, and the
earth produced its fruit. (James 5:16b-19)

In II Timothy 3:15, Paul reminds us of our other bulwark for our children: "and from childhood you have known the sacred writings which are able to give you the wisdom that leads to salvation through faith which is in Christ Jesus."

I am acquainted with some parents who started to pray for the future spouses of their children when their children were born. There they were, their babies in their arms, praying for other children, unknown to them, in an unknown place on the globe, who would someday become their sons and daughters-in-law. They were praying for dedicated Christian mates for their children. In faith, they continued their prayer over the course of their children's growing up. Essentially, they were praying for an alleviation of possible future stress for their children.

In later chapters, specific guidance will be presented on *what,* exactly, we should teach our children and *how* we should teach our children in order to help them develop strength of character, wisdom, insight, and the courage to manage adversity and stress. One of the key steps in doing this is to pray for our children. But then a question arises. "What, exactly, do I pray for? Do I pray that my children won't have adversity? We already know that adversity is inescapable. We also know that adversity can be good for our children. So what's left to pray for?"

God's Word gives specific things that parents can pray for to help their children stand strong in the face of negative stress. These Scriptures were offered by the spiritual "parents" of the first Christians, who were in many ways like children, and who faced more severe stress than modern children will ever face. Indeed, the apostles even referred to their readers as "children," which makes their prayers even more appropriate for our children than we could possibly imagine.

Any of these prayers can be prayed with confidence and certainty:

1. Colossians 1:9-14.
2. Philippians 1:9-11.
3. Ephesians 1:5-19a.

These prayers for godly wisdom and guidance are a critical component of the first line of defense that parents provide for our children against destructive stress.

BUT I HAVE NO FORMAL EDUCATION!

Even if we have things clearly spelled out for us, many of us still hesitate to take action. We are, after all, products of the society, the culture, and the times in which we live. One of the tendencies of human behavior is to believe blindly in the "experts"—the educators, the psychologists, the counselors, and the professors—knowing they are trained, and we are not. The fact is that, oftentimes, people with specialized training do have *some* answers. They have *some* good advice. But they do not have *all* of the answers. And they do not have a monopoly on all of the good advice.

I am a trained professional, but if there is one thing I could persuade parents to do, it would be to look first to God's wisdom for guidance in developing the kinds of skills, insights, and abilities needed in helping children manage stress. The real starting point is very simple. It is the same starting point we use in managing our own stress.[1] Immerse yourself in the Word of God. Study the Scriptures. Learn from Christian counselors. If you do this, God promises special blessings to parents.

1. Strong confidence (Proverbs 14:26).
2. Understanding (Proverbs 9:10).
3. Good (Proverbs 16:20; Romans 8:28-29).
4. Security and a refuge (Proverbs 30:5).
5. Decision-making ability (Proverbs 3:5-6).
6. Guidance/correction (II Timothy 3:16-17).
7. Joy, restoration, enlightened judgment (Psalm 19:7-9).

Obviously, there are many others. These are only a few. We can all benefit from considering the advice of earthly experts. Proverbs 15:22 encourages us to get counsel. But our first source of advice should be God's Word. Our second source of expertise should be counselors who submit to the authority of God's Word. God has promised to give us insight in raising our children. Be confident. He will not let us down.

Questions for Parents

1. How would you apply Proverbs 2, Ephesians 6:4, and Colossians 3:21 to your home? Be specific.

2. According to the above verses, how would you define your primary role in helping your children manage stress?

3. What specific things can you do to help your children develop their sense of self-worth and self-confidence?

4. How can you strengthen your child's belief system?

5. How would you apply Deuteronomy 6:1-7, 20-21, 24-25 to your home?

Questions for Children and Parents

1. Read Colossians 1:9-14 together. Talk about it. Write out how that prayer can be applied to specific things your child faces.

2. Read Philippians 1:9-11 together. Talk about it. Ask your child(ren) to explain what that means and express it in specific terms relating to his everyday life.

3. Read Ephesians 1:15-91a together. Talk about it. Ask your child(ren) how those verses can help them face problems.

*SPECIAL NOTE:

The March 17, 1988 *Rocky Mountain News* reported that David Shannon's record will be cleared. Procedures are underway to reinstate David Shannon at the U.S. Air Force Academy. His father, Paul, said, "It took about 1200 hours of my time and a tremendous amount of money. If I hadn't quit my job back east and come out here, I couldn't have done it. But my son was never guilty and you have to fight for your kids when they're right, you know."

On May 3, 1989, *The Denver Post* reported that David Shannon had been cleared of all charges. *The Post* article said, "Shannon and his father, Paul Shannon, 53, waged a three-year battle with academy officials and Air Force top brass in the Pentagon after young Shannon was dismissed for lying in May 1985, two week before graduation. . . . Paul Shannon, owner of a Security hardware store, estimates he's spent $25,000 in travel costs to Washington and other expenses and about 1,200 hours fighting to clear his son's name."

[1] Arnold H. Burron, and Jerry Crews, *Guaranteed Steps to Managing Stress* (Wheaton, Ill.: Tyndale House Publishers, 1986), p. 214.

CHAPTER THREE

Signs and Sources of Stress

"I HAVE A STOMACHACHE, MOMMY," Ian complained for the third time that week.

"Well, where does it hurt, dear?"

"I don't know. It just hurts!"

"Do you think you should stay home from school?"

"Yes."

"Maybe we should go to the doctor."

"No! I don't need to go to the doctor."

"But, honey, I'm worried about how often you've been sick lately. I think we should go to the doctor."

"No, Mommy. I don't feel that bad. I just think I'll feel better if I stay home from school and rest for awhile."

"All right," Ian's concerned mother decided, "But if you don't feel better tomorrow, we're going to the doctor."

"OK," Ian agreed, a note of relief in his voice.

Ian's mother knit her brow in concern at the many different illnesses her son had been experiencing. Last week he was plagued by a sore throat—and now these stomachaches. What was causing him to feel ill so often?

Ever since the Tolbeys had moved to a new town, Carol, their nine-year-old daughter, had been throwing uncharacteristic temper-tantrums. The usually amiable and cheerful girl had been showing drastic mood swings which confused and worried her anxious parents. They were baffled by her sudden behavioral changes. Their daughter had become a serious behavior problem.

Although fictitious, these two stories have thousands of parallels in reality, and they serve to demonstrate how complex the symptoms of stress in children can be. Two important keys in unlocking the door of understanding regarding stress in children are determining the *source* of the stress, and understanding the *symptoms* of stress. This chapter addresses these two important factors.

Sources of stress are listed only briefly in this chapter since they are discussed in detail, along with what to do about them, throughout this book. Before looking at a list of such sources, however, several important points should be kept in mind:

1.) What is a source of severe stress for one child may not be as severe for another child.

2.) What "experts" tell us are sources of stress may not reflect reality. For example, for many years, experts have been telling adults that the fear of nuclear war is a source of stress to children. Some experts have gone even further, and have suggested that much of the destructive, self-serving, "me-first," pleasure-seeking value system of adolescents and young people in the eighties is a direct result of such fear, and that the fear of nuclear war gave rise to an eat-drink-and-be-merry-for-tomorrow-we-die philosophy.

But in surveys of college students I have conducted, students in the early 1980s, who would be logically identified as the group most likely exposed to the "nuclear-holocaust" scare of the sixties and seventies, without one exception did not report that they were ever anxious about the threat of nuclear war! Some students who had participated in school "bomb drills" reported, in retrospect, that, not only was there no fear or anxiety about nuclear war, but they had no real grasp of why they had to periodically hide under their desks or crouch against the wall. Many enjoyed the activity!

The point here is that before you assume that some incident or source is stressful you should take time to evaluate your own child. One has to wonder how much stress adults impose upon children by unnecessarily exposing them to the fact that there are uncontrollable phenomena which cause stress for adults! Take care, then, to really observe and listen to your child. Don't assume, as in the case of the Challenger space shuttle tragedy in 1986, that such an event calls for an invasion of the school classroom by a battalion of psychologists, counselors, and other "helping professionals," who in reality may be projecting upon children their own anxieties! What stresses adults may not stress children. Conversely, some things that cause stress for some children, may not cause stress for some adults.

3.) Be aware that, even among children in the same family, reactions to stress and sources of stress may differ among brothers and sisters. If five-year-old Keith sobs in terror at the prospect of entering the "Tadpoles" class at the local community swimming pool and his six-year-old sister, Charah, has to be restrained from gleefully plunging into the deep end, there is nothing wrong with Keith. He is just different from his sister, and his difference should be respected.

SOURCES OF STRESS

Dr. Ellis Copeland, of the University of Northern Colorado, prepared a study of different questionnaires which purported to measure stress in adolescents.[1] Dr. Copeland's research noted, among other points, that "most adolescents report school problems more often than any other form of psycho-social stress." Specific sources of stress for adolescents which were included on more than one of the questionnaires evaluated in the study, are summarized and categorized below. These should be viewed, however, within the context of the guidelines with which this chapter began. Therefore, they are not listed here in order of significance.

Sources of Stress for Adolescents

1. Death of a family member, relative, or friend.
2. Divorce or separation of parents.
3. Conflict in the home.
4. Geographical move to a new home or to a new school.
5. Problems experienced by parents, such as socio-economic changes, substance abuse, illness, etc.
6. Problems, or dramatic changes experienced by siblings, including pregnancy, discipline problems, leaving home, and so on.
7. Interpersonal relationships, including making and keeping friends, dating, problems with authority figures such as teachers.
8. Physical problems, including "appearance" problems such as acne, braces, glasses; and "body image" problems, as well as self-concept problems.
9. Performance pressures: job, school, sports, homework, and other demands on time and effort.
10. Substance abuse.
11. Changes in oneself: such as, physical and perceptual changes through stages of puberty.

Interestingly, not one of these scales elicited responses pertaining to sex or to sex drive, but sex drive and questions of sexual morality constitute a consistent source of stress for most adolescents. Sex and sexual morality, for example, are of particular concern to children with rigid value systems, and that includes Christian children. Specific sources of help that specifically, and thoroughly, address sexual problems of teenagers should be consulted by Christian parents. Any well-stocked Christian bookstore can provide excellent resources. Under no circumstances should parents allow the school sex-education program to be the sole source of information on this important topic.

Sources of Stress for Young Children

In addition to most of the sources identified above, young children can experience stress from the following circumstances or phenomena.

1. Fear of the dark.
2. Fear of animals, especially biting animals.
3. Fear of strangers.
4. Fear of school. (Research indicates that one out of twenty children can be "school-phobic.")
5. Fear of ghosts, monsters, or other imaginary horror figures.
6. Fear of traveling alone.
7. Fear of abandonment—which includes fear of the death of a parent or loved one.
8. Loss of a loved one.
9. Loss of a pet.
10. Fear of failure.

Later in this chapter, specific methods of responding to childhood fears will be discussed, while throughout the book, other stress-reducing approaches will be presented. Let's turn, now, to signs of stress in children.

SYMPTOMS OF STRESS

There are several warning signals which a child will display when he is under stress. Aside from prevention of stress, recognizing and acting upon these symptoms is the most important step in alleviating childhood stress. Some of the symptoms of stress are very subtle, while others are quite blatant. The following is a list of common symptoms of stress:

1. Bed-wetting.
2. Stuttering.
3. Frequent complaints of "I don't feel well."
4. Insomnia.
5. High anxiety.
6. Drop in performance at school.
7. Discipline infractions, including talking back, rule-breaking, defying authority, fighting, and other forms of disobedience.

Other symptoms of stress include accident proneness and other attention-getting behavior, such as incessant crying, screaming, or deliberate disobedience. All of these are symptoms of stress in a child who is not too timid to misbehave in a deliberate manner to get attention. Moodiness and irritability, such as we saw in the example of Carol's behavior in the beginning of the chapter, are indications that a child is experiencing more stress than he can handle alone. The child may be so preoccupied with something in his life which is not right that he does not have the energy or the desire to maintain an amicable character. This behavior is common in adults, also, for how often do we become irritable when the demands placed upon us are too great?

Frequent complaints of, "I don't feel well," are an example of an avoidance ploy which children may use when under stress. Many children (and adults!) have a tendency to try to ignore a problem and hope it will go away rather than face the problem and deal with it. Therefore, children will pretend that they don't feel well so that they may stay home, a place where the problem, perhaps, cannot reach them. One of the most frequent complaints of illness is the infamous "stomachache." Children are very clever in using this excuse for one reason: it cannot be checked. How can one gauge the severity of a stomachache without experiencing it for one's self? If a child were to complain of a cold, he would cough or sniffle. If she were to complain of a fever, she would, of course, feel warm. If he had a sore throat, he would have a hard time swallowing, or his throat would appear raw. But a stomachache—who can tell, by looking, that something is wrong? One must be cautious, however, when dealing with a child who frequently complains of illness, to determine that he is not really sick. As with any recurring illness, the child should be given a thorough medical examination whether he wants it or not. (*Children should not be allowed to determine when a doctor's visit is necessary. You must insist upon a medical examination if you are concerned, regardless of what the child says.*)

Insomnia, high anxiety, and a drop in performance at school are also symptoms that a child's attention is not focused where it should be. If a child's preoccupation with something is keeping his mind from the activities of daily life, then that "something" has become so dominating in the child's eyes that he cannot function in a normal manner. As with frequent complaints of illness, however, a child experiencing insomnia should be thoroughly checked by a physician.

Probably the most important step one can take in recognizing symptoms of stress is to *know your child* well enough to notice any changes in behavior—no matter how slight. If you take time to get to know the characteristics of your child, you will probably not see any of the symptoms of stress which indicate that he is experiencing a lack of attention. Why? Because, in getting to know your child, you are giving her the attention she needs!

CALMING THE FEARS OF VERY YOUNG CHILDREN

Fears common to very young children constitute a unique source of stress. Several specific steps to follow in helping your young child deal with fears are presented in this chapter. These suggestions are the work of Dr. T. Berry Brazelton, M.D., and first appeared in Family Circle (8/1/86, p. 103).

Six Ways to Ease Your Child's Fears

1. Respect what your child tells you about his fear. Look under the bed or in the closet with him, showing him that no monsters are lurking there.

2. Let him know that it's natural at his age to be worried about certain things. Assure him that, although they seem frightening now, he will learn how to handle them.

3. Support him as he struggles with his fears. Let him regress, be dependent and act like a baby. He won't want to do it for long. Even as you hold him, he'll start to squirm away. Then compliment him for being so "grown up."

4. Reassure him that all children have fears. Tell him about your own fears at his age and how you overcame them.

5. When he conquers a fear, point this out to him so

he can learn from his success. You can refer back
to it when new fears arise.

6. If his fears begin to invade his life, if the same fear
lasts beyond six months, or if fearfulness is
affecting his capacity to make friends, seeking
professional guidance. A crippling or persistent
fear can be a child's way of crying out for help.

To these suggestions, I would add the character
development steps and personal strength development
suggestions in chapter six, as well as the reminder that
consistent spiritual training is the best method of preventing
childhood fears, some of which may be parent-induced! If
parents are careless, children can develop fears. For example, is
it any wonder that preschoolers who are exposed to grotesque
video images, including symbolic bestiality, sadomasochism,
decapitation, sexually perverse stimulation, heavy metal
"music," and other assaults on their immature senses are
tormented by nebulous fears of the unknown?

Contrast the fears of such children with the tractable and
confident disposition of a toddler whose parents follow a
predictable nighttime regimen that includes playing such
music as "Kids Sing Praise!"[2] — a collection of songs by
children—prayer, and maybe a Bible story.

Just as confidence is parent induced through careful
planning, fears are induced through careless planning!

The best method of dealing with stress or fears? An
awareness of the fact that parents must not be the source of
them through carelessness and that children whose faith in
God is nurtured will have a *supernatural response* to fear.

Questions for Parents

1. What kinds of adult stress do you feel you may have imposed upon your child(ren)?

2. If you have more than one child, give two examples of how they differ from each other? How would these differences affect their sources of stress?

3. List any major sources of stress in your family over the past year.

   How have you or can you help your child face these specific stresses?

4. Examine your own attitudes, worries, and fears. Have you transferred any of these to your children?

Questions for Children and Parents

1. Children: What things cause you the most anxiety, worry, or fear?

2. Do you think it is all right to be afraid? Read Isaiah 41:10. What does God say about fear?

3. Parent: Discuss your child's fears in regard to your fears at his age. What were your fears?

4. Discuss how television, books, or friends' conversation may be creating or encouraging this type of stress. Write out a single statement outlining it and then one describing how to overcome it.

[1] Ellis P. Copeland, "Assessing Adolescent Stress by Questionnaire: An Evaluation of Methods," an address to NASP, 1985.

[2] "Kids Sing Praise," Brentwood Records, Inc., © 1986. P.O. Box 1028, Brentwood, TN 37027

CHAPTER FOUR

Reducing Stress at Home

"As far back as I can remember," the speaker said, "my dad had what he called 'The Jar.'"

We were sharing memories of tough times in our childhoods, when layoffs and scarce jobs reflected on a personal scale the impact of a national recession. Those were the days when families were short of money and when, in many households, the financial stresses faced by struggling young parents filtered through to tender young ears in late-night, muffled, worried conversations.

"I can remember how some of the kids at school worried," the speaker continued, "when their dads lost their jobs, or when they had to move in with relatives, and 'do without' in a lot of painful ways. But the funny thing is," he said, "I was never really concerned because I was in on a family secret: *The Jar*. I was probably five or six," he confided, "and I can remember this like it was yesterday. One night, after we finished a supper which had culminated in a discussion about the hard times that seemed to have overtaken every family we knew, Dad beckoned my brother and sister and me to come with him. He wanted to show us something.

"We had one of those old basements that seemed dank

and gloomy no matter what you did, and we followed Dad tentatively down the creaky steps. What I remember most is the sudden coolness and the musty smell—but anyway—Dad crossed the basement and gently wiggled a loose stone. In a soft voice, which seemed to be a special, mysterious whisper, he said to us, 'I want you kids to know what I have here, just in case anything should happen to me.' With that, Dad reached into the hole in the wall and pulled out a plain glass jar. We could hear coins jingling, and we could see some paper money in the jar—how much there was, I didn't know at the time, and I don't know for sure to this day—but to a child, whatever was hidden in a hole in a stone wall just had to be a fortune!

"'Every once in a while,' Dad conspiratorially confessed, 'If I have extra money, I put it in The Jar. Then, if we're ever short of money, I can come down to the jar. I don't ever want you to touch the jar,' he solemnly admonished us, 'or tell anyone about it, but I do want you to know that it's here. And if anything ever happens to me, you remind mom about where it is.'"

The speaker paused, as if lost in another time and another place. No one interrupted. More quietly now, as if sharing a deep secret, he continued.

"Times stayed tough for a long time. As we matured, we were able to observe clues about our financial status. I can remember Mom coming up with some creative meals with so few ingredients that you'd think she was a magician. The kids at school expressed their anxieties, and a lot of hard-working, respectable people were on welfare. But we kids never seemed to worry. Whenever an expression of serious need would come up—and that was rare, but it usually came up at the supper table—Dad would lean back, look very thoughtful, and then quietly pronounce, with the firm conviction of a head of state, 'Well, I suppose I'll have to go to The Jar.' It was as though the Lord had provided a private little emergency fund, just for our family. And over the years, every extreme financial emergency would evoke the same behavior. Dad would lean back. He would ponder pensively for what seemed like interminable minutes. Then he would look intently at Mom with a reassuring gaze. And then would come the decision. 'Well,' he would decide, 'I suppose I'll have to go to The Jar.' And we kids always felt almost palpable relief: We knew the Lord had enabled Dad to have The Jar. Our family wasn't broke.

"But here's the strangest part of the story," the speaker declared. "Of course, since Dad had admonished us with great solemnity never to disturb the stone or the jar, and since we were privy to his special secret, we respected his warning. We never talked about, or touched, the jar. We only knew the great secret was there. And we knew that, in extreme emergency, Dad would 'go to The Jar.' It wasn't until years later, when times of prosperity had come back and when Dad was comfortably retired, that Mom shared the real secret of The Jar. Neither she—nor we—knew at some of the times of most need in our family's circumstances, there was not much more than a dollar or two in Dad's jar. You see, it was Dad's quiet confidence that dispelled our worries. That was the real treasure of The Jar."

AN ATMOSPHERE OF SECURITY

Many specific things can be done to minimize, or to avoid altogether, much of the stress that children encounter on the home front. A number of specific suggestions are discussed in the second part of this chapter. None of these activities or specific suggestions, though, can be effective if there is not an *atmosphere of security in the home*.

Providing that atmosphere of security is a challenging task. "Atmosphere" is, after all, very abstract. Consider for example, atmosphere in a restaurant. One restaurant may spend thousands of dollars on interior decorating; they may hire the finest chef available, and their fare may be the most nutritious and delicious food in town. Nevertheless, people may flock to a competitor whose surroundings are much less pretentious, whose food is "good," but not outstanding, whose chef is a cook, and whose entrees are, perhaps, even more expensive, solely because its patrons are drawn by the "atmosphere." They might not be able to tell you specifically what it is; they might not even say that is what attracts them, but when preferences are articulated, it comes down to atmosphere.

The same, indefinable, vital, mood-creating and mood-sustaining quality can prevail in a home.

CREATING AN ATMOSPHERE OF SECURITY

Since "atmosphere" is so hard to describe and an atmosphere of stress-minimizing security is so difficult to define, what we are after can be best illustrated with the following stories.

One of the listeners to the story told at the outset of this chapter shared his insights into how his own concept of self-worth and his feeling of security was developed.

"I can remember when money was short at our house, too," he reminisced. "The main social event for Mom was to go to Ladies Guild at church. That was fine. It didn't cost anything, and it was her 'night out.' But the real big deal for Dad was his bowling night. I can remember the folks discussing expenses, and I can still hear Mom insisting that Dad go bowling—that he worked hard, that he deserved it, that he didn't spend money on smoking or drinking, and that, no matter where the family would have to cut corners, Dad would go bowling. And I remember that Dad reluctantly succumbed to Mom's persuasion. Bowling was, after all, his claim to recognition. It was a cherished passion with him.

"One day, not too long after the 'bowling' decision," the

speaker continued, "the family—Mom, Dad, my sister, and I—all went to the county fair. 'Just to look around,' Dad had said, 'and maybe to get some cotton candy.' It was the *only* thing we could afford at the fair. Well, we got to the fair, and after the cotton candy and plenty of gawking at everything, we stumbled across this quaint old guy with a couple of horses hitched to this antique buggy. He was selling rides—a quick trip into the past—down the dirt road that wended its way through the big cottonwoods that hugged the riverbank, and back to the fairgrounds. We kids had never seen anything like this, and our fascination could have given us open-mouthed lockjaw. The horses were snorting and stomping at the flies, tails flicking like huge, braided whips. To us, the whole scene was a page right out of history.

"I guess I really didn't notice, at first, that Dad was talking intently to the owner of the rig. Sis and I were too busy admiring the horses. The next thing I remember is sitting on this velvet seat, Dad in the middle, Sis on one side and me on the other, certainly—in our minds at least—the envy of every kid at the fair. And I remember Mom's reaction. "But honey," she protested, "that was your bowling money!"

"It's okay, dear," my dad replied, his eyes twinkling with that special kind of insight only a few gentle souls possess. "I didn't give up a bowling night. I'm building a memory for our kids."

The listeners were silent.

There was a long pause. "It's funny," the speaker reflected. "Dad was, indeed, building a memory. But not the one he thought he was building. Sure, I remember the ride, and so does my sister. But what we both remember most is Dad's sacrifice for us and his good intentions. I have a memory of that day. It's a memory of a dad who thought that Sis and I were more special than anything, and that he

57

was ready to sacrifice something important to him just for us. "Yep," he murmured softly, more to himself than to the rest of us, "Dad was building memories, all right."

OTHER "ATMOSPHERE" BUILDERS

What do you remember from your childhood that made you feel that your home and your relationships were particularly secure? Sadly, most adults have no memories of security. Their lives were filled with stress, conflict, and anxiety. They did not feel secure within their homes. They felt no security in their relationships. But of those adults who can look back with fond memories on a feeling of security at home, a feeling that things were under control, and that they were in a safe environment, specific incidents stand out.

A twenty-year-old, poised, self-confident student shared with me her perception of her father, a man in his forties. "Whenever I think of my dad, I always get this picture in my mind of him reading the Bible. Sure, I see him playing ball with us, mowing the lawn, and other stuff, but if I unexpectedly think of him, I see him reading the Bible. It gives me a good feeling . . . like, he's solid, you know . . . dependable."

Another student, an equally poised, confident young lady, shared how her family, after the evening meal, would always have a family prayer. She shared how her parents would often pray for specific friends in need and that they would always conclude with this petition: ". . . And show us, Lord, what each of us has to offer, that can help our friends." She always felt good, she said, knowing that she, herself, might be asked by her parents to offer a telephone call, the running of an errand, a prayer, a visit, or something else within the realm of her ability to contribute, to share a family friend's burden.

". . . He who has lost his life for My sake," Jesus said in Matthew 10:39, "shall find it." Security, for this young lady, lay in self-sacrifice and in serving others as though serving the Lord Jesus Himself.

"Looking back," she mused, "I have to say that the most important thing I learned was that other people have problems and that we share and bear one another's burdens. My problems—my stresses, as we term it—seemed surmountable. I didn't feel alone in my problems. Others had them also. And others were there to help me." She added, with an afterthought that was, perhaps, the most salient point of all, "When you are helping somebody else, you don't have time to dwell on your own problems and let them get you down."

ATMOSPHERE: WHAT GOES INTO IT?

An atmosphere of security in the home is, perhaps, the most significant contributor to reducing stress for a child at home. But the influence of an atmosphere of security extends far beyond the home; children take security with them when they feel personally secure.

Although the atmosphere we've been talking about is difficult to define and although it is difficult to lay out specific steps to follow to achieve such an atmosphere, the examples we have looked at do provide us with certain insights. These insights can help any parent create his own atmosphere of security at home.

The examples had these elements in common:

1. Parents in the examples did not reveal their own anxieties to their children. If they were anxious, they took those anxieties to the Lord and reflected an attitude of confidence and security to their children, a confidence and security that directly reflected their faith in Christ.
2. The parents showed that they were ready and willing to help others; they put others' needs before their own needs or desires.

59

3. The parents showed that they valued their children. They did this through:

a) putting their children's needs before their own;

b) asking their children for their contributions—no matter how small—to solving friends' problems;

c) touching, hugging, and otherwise showing affection;

d) taking time to listen, talk, explain and ask forgiveness.

4. The parents showed that they were well-grounded. They, themselves, were an example of stability. This was particularly illustrated in the example of the daughter's image of her father seeking spiritual wisdom in the Bible.

5. Each family member's feelings were important. Privacy was respected, even for the youngest person in the family.

6. Interpersonal relationships were cultivated and cherished. There was "networking": an expanded family—made up of relatives and cherished friends—asserted its place in the household.

7. There was a feeling of "we," "us," and "our," an ownership and sharing of triumphs and problems that was plural. "I," "me," and "mine" were minimized. There was no feeling of being alone or isolated.

What memories do you have of your own feelings of security at home? What significant element created your sense of security?

Any parent can incorporate any of the elements above, as well as those from his or her own memory bank, into special experiences uniquely suited to his or her own household. Atmosphere, most assuredly, isn't the only element in reducing stress on the home front; but an atmosphere of security is an indispensable and necessary prerequisite to establishing specific steps to reduce stress at home.

Let's turn, now, to specifics that can be put into place once an atmosphere of security has been established.

REDUCING STRESS ON THE HOME FRONT

Wanda and Dave are two young parents who sought help for their stress at home. Joel and Michael, their two preschoolers (ages four and three), were giving them fits. Every morning was the same: fighting between the boys, whining, and general crankiness. Since their apartment was small, it wasn't possible to "send the kids to the playroom," and, so to speak, banish the crankiness and the conflict to the confines of the kids' room.

In this case, the source of the problem was easy to find. Dave had been raised in an extremely strict environment. Until he was well into his teens, he was totally dominated by a well-intentioned but autocratic father who allowed him no freedom whatsoever. A backlash was almost inevitable. So when Dave became a parent, he became a "laissez-faire" parent. He used repeated verbal expressions of displeasure when Joel and Michael misbehaved but without ever imposing any sort of consequences for misbehavior or disobedience. His voice grew louder and louder as his directives were ignored, and, in turn, the children became louder and louder in their conflicts and their demands. Raucous noisiness was a common condition in Dave and Wanda's household, to the point that Wanda retreated to an already overly loud television set or created an escape by feeling constantly sleepy. Dave's continuing refusal to, in Wanda's words, "take charge," was a constant source of irritation to her and led to her being the disciplinarian, often to the point of overreacting to the boys' misbehavior. When Wanda finally decided to seek outside counsel, her pleas for help was motivated by fear. Her state of stress had become so acute and her emotions so out of control that she was afraid she would end up venting her anger on Joel and Michael—in a moment of extreme emotion, in a physically abusive way. The fact that child abuse had already occurred in her household, in the form of a chaotic and stress-filled environment caused by a total lack of structure, had escaped her husband completely. Fortunately, she had the good sense to stifle her pride and to admit that she and Dave needed help.

CAUSES OF STRESS IN THE HOME

We have seen how important an atmosphere of security is in the home. It builds a calm, resolute, and peaceful disposition in a child which will help him approach stressful situations with confidence.

On the other hand, there are specific conditions that impose stress on children when they are at home.

1. A lack of agreement between parents on how to raise and discipline their children;
2. Interference with parental discipline by any other authority figure (grandpa, grandma, sister-in-law, etc.) who is usually or frequently in the home;
3. A lack of consistency in discipline, to the point that, one time a child may be disciplined for something and the next time he may blatantly get away with it;
4. A lack of clear-cut, well-explained expectations for children on "do's" and "don'ts" for their behavior;
5. A lack of well-defined expectations for children on what will happen to them if they "do" the "don'ts" or "don't" do the "do's";
6. Open quarreling between parents or other significant adults;

7. Tolerated quarreling among children;

8. A lack of any kind of routine in the home: no set time or procedure for family mealtimes; no set bedtimes; nothing that can be counted on, or expected, as something that is consistent;

9. Poor diet, irregular meals, poor nutrition;

10. Exposure to inappropriate entertainment or education stimuli. (Violence, sex, sustained intense suspense, horror, or even non-violent, non-pornographic adult material.) For example, one six year old, normal in every way, became very upset watching a "forties" television movie in which the star became ill by overeating a forbidden treat. Another child, after watching a Christmas classic about a man who becomes invisible by wishing he had never been born, suffered recurrent nightmares about not being visible to those who loved him, reliving, in his dreams, the trauma experienced by the character in the movie;

11. Being teased, ridiculed, humiliated, or taunted. A child has no defenses against such sarcasm and verbal assaults;

12. Having too little responsibility, or having too much responsibility, for family chores;

13. Being expected to be just like some other child: an older sibling, a family friend, or another high achiever or "good behaver."

Each of these causes of stress in the home implies its own solutions. Some additional thoughts connected with each of these solutions, though, can help.

REDUCING STRESS IN THE HOME

The most important step parents can take in removing stress in the home, indeed, an indispensable step we cannot do without, is outlined in detail in chapter six. Several other significant steps for removing stress are presented here, but chapter six is vital. And life changing.

There are, however, some steps that are easy to take.

Step 1. *(If you are a single parent, decide firmly upon these items.) Agree, with your partner, in as much detail as possible, on the following items:*

a. The main goal you have in raising your children. (See chapter 1.)

b. What you will and will not tolerate in the way of specific behavior. You will, then, not create stress by making spur-of-the-moment decisions in response to unexpected requests or situations. Obviously, anything that detracts from the main goal should not be tolerated. Also, contrary to what the "experts" might say, you are the final authority in your home. You have a right to cultivate behavior that will contribute to peace and quiet for everyone in your home. You, after all, are the "climate control"—the thermostat, if you will—primarily responsible for the emotional warmth in your home.

c. What the consequences of inappropriate behavior will be.

As a Christian parent, you have been charged by God to administer discipline. Several Scriptures give clear guidance on God's commands regarding parental discipline.

From the very beginning of the Bible, God spoke of parental discipline. When talking about Abraham, God said, "For I have chosen him, in order that he may command his children and his household after him to keep the way of the Lord by doing righteousness and justice" (Genesis 18:19)

Parents are also given a means to shape their children's behavior from the very beginning of life. How? By instilling a love and fear of the Lord. Deuteronomy 4:9-10 speaks of God's statutes and the obedience He requires of His children. "Only give heed to yourself and keep your soul diligently, lest you forget the things which your eyes have seen, and lest they depart from your heart all the days of your life; but make them known to your sons and your grandsons. Remember the day you stood before the Lord your God at Horeb, when the Lord said to me, 'Assemble the people to Me, that I may let them hear My words so they may learn to fear Me all the days they live on the earth, and that they may teach their children.'"

And when Moses had finished speaking to the people of Israel, just before they crossed into the promised land, he told them, "Take to your heart all the words with which I am warning you today, which you shall command your sons to observe carefully, even all the words of this law" (Deuteronomy 32:46).

To those verbal commands and instructions a parents must give his children, especially regarding obedience to the Lord, is added the warning, "Whom the Lord loves He reproves, Even as a father the son in whom he delights" (Proverbs 3:12). Proverbs 13:24 tells parents, "He who spares his rod hates his son, but he who loves him disciplines him diligently." Proverbs 22:15 gives this strong word on discipline: "Foolishness is bound up in the heart of a child; The rod of discipline will remove it far from him."

Several other verses in Proverbs command discipline. Ephesians 6:4 gives added dimension to the subject of discipline. "And, fathers, do not provoke your children to anger; but bring them up in the discipline and instruction of the Lord." Other verses such as Colossians 3:21, I Timothy 3:4, Titus 1:6, and Hebrews 12:7 give more encouragement to honest, godly discipline. Do not be afraid to mold your child's behavior by appropriate consequences to disobedience.

There is currently a major movement across the country against corporal punishment. One social worker, investigating a Christian father for physical abuse after he spanked his thirteen-year-old child, admitted in an unguarded moment, "I know how tough it can be. My teenage is absolutely incorrigible. I don't know what to do with her!" Incredibly, she was invested with the responsibility—without further investigation—of counseling the Christian parents about what Social Services said was inappropriate discipline: a spanking which their rebellious teenager charged was abusive!

Another Christian parent, faced with a rebellious teenager who had been promised corporal punishment if he messed with drugs, told my radio audience one day that he telephones the Social Service agency ahead of time to send out a representative to observe the spanking. He anticipates that his child might do what is the current rage among many contemporary adolescents: call Social Services or the police and report the parents for child abuse!

Remember your primary goal. Be flexible. Ask the Lord for guidance. And establish consequences. Do not seek input from secular experts whose advice runs contrary to Scripture. Clear-cut, known consequences and discipline which is biblically guided and according to the parent's word is not harmful to your child. To the contrary, boundaries and discipline create security for a child. It reduces the stress of uncertainty, not only about wrong actions, but also about the quality, depth, and commitment of a parent's love.

If you need counsel, seek *Christian* counsel. There are many factual examples of "experts" who conduct workshops in child rearing who follow their unscriptural, modernistic advice and whose own children are totally out of control.

    d. Agree upon the administration of discipline. Both parents have a responsibility to discipline their children. One of the worst forms of stress to impose on a child is the "wait until your father gets home" variety, or the, "I wonder if Mom (or Dad) will find out." A devastating stress to inflict upon your child is an argument he or she observes between adults about what to do in a discipline situation.

The parent closest to the situation, in time or in physical proximity, should administer the discipline. Consequences are lost on very young children if discipline is delayed or postponed. Anxiety and stress become a problem for many children who must anticipate the impending wrath of a parent who will discipline them "later."

Think for a moment. If your child needed love in the form of a hug, a touch, a kiss, or a word of reassurance, would you say, "Wait until your father (or mother) gets home"? If your child needs love in the form of discipline, it, too, should be readily given.

In some families, parents ask that, in the absence of the parents, any adult—grandpa, grandma, uncle, aunt, or other respected elder—administer necessary discipline. This means parents must have clear goals, expectations, and established consequences. Insist that other parties respect your forms of discipline so that your child gets consistent loving discipline from all significant elders in his life. If Jesus Christ is the true Head of your household, such shared, loving discipline is a highly desirable condition.

In Mark 3:25, Jesus declared, "And if a house is divided against itself, that house will not be able to stand." Agreement and consistency on all the points cited above is a vital step in reducing the assault of stress upon the children in your home.

Step 2. *Let your children know, very clearly, what you expect of them, and what the consequences of disobedience are.*

One of the most common sources of stress on the job for adults is *ambiguity of expectations.* Simply, what constitutes satisfactory performance is not clearly spelled out. Uncertainty—a lack of clear-cut tasks, a lack of rules, or a lack of clear expectations—creates stress. In repeated experiments, research at the college level consistently shows that, when provided with a choice between pursuing independent work with self-created goals and non-specific, ambiguous standards, or the completion of work within stringently-defined criteria, virtually 100% of subjects sacrificed freedom with ambiguity and chose the security of well-defined expectations. In various ways, the stress of uncertainty is identified as the reason for their choice. Children also need and appreciate limits and clear expectations. It reduces their stress.

Step 3. *Closely related to the stress of ambiguity is the stress of a lack of structure or routine in the home.*

One example will suffice.

Denise is a single parent who quite profitably freelances a variety of secretarial skills in her home. Some "rush" jobs require that she work through mealtimes. Sometimes her early-elementary grade-school children get the old standby, peanut butter and jelly sandwiches, for supper. An occasional missed or "junk food" meal would not be a problem if Denise and her children had some routine. Denise, however, has no desirable bedtime routine, either. Her children, ages six, seven, and nine, habitually fall asleep in front of the television set, the last impressions in their young minds usually some surrealistic, sadomasochistic rock video assault leaping out of the screen into the living room. About the only consistent routine is the typical late night hassle of Denise waking the children to go to bed. Sometimes, prior to falling asleep, the children fight over which channel to watch. Oftentimes, they are overly tired, cranky, and lethargic in the morning; there is constant bickering and whining. There is stress for Denise, stress for her children, and, unfortunately, stress at school.[1]

The solution? The simple step of establishing a known bedtime hour, an evening Bible story, a family prayer, and Denise's consistent follow through would eliminate the stresses above.

A disturbing lack of routine includes: times when children have to postpone or miss a favored activity, or when they must interrupt an activity at an inopportune time; being scolded for failing to anticipate an adult's timetable; being late for a required activity (such as a meal), and feeling that things are not in control, that the unexpected will intrude at any moment. Routine, however minimal, provides a sense of predictability and security.

Step 4. *Avoid quarreling, fighting, or other forms of bitterness or anger, including pouting, sulking, sarcasm, or noncommunication.*

Tracy and Ned live in a large city, over a thousand miles from either of their families except for Tracy's brother and his wife who are in virtually the same predicament. Curiously, though, the two families do not associate with one another, except on holidays, and then on only very superficial terms, even though each family privately prizes family ties. The reason? Over two decades earlier, their children, who were then toddlers, were allowed to fight, without any adult intervention. Squabbles between Tracy and Ned's eighteen-month-old and their relatives' two-year-old over a toy, a book, or an area of space were allowed to proceed because no adult had the good sense or the courage to intervene! Tracy's brother Mel stubbornly insisted that children had to learn to "fight it out," "fend for themselves," and "solve their own problems." Astoundingly, no adult, including spouses, Grandpa, or Grandma, challenged Mel when he asserted the dogma that the parents "shouldn't treat the kids like babies!"—as if an eighteen month old and a two year old were anything but babies!

So "fight it out" the children did, as did the toddlers who came after them, creating many a scene, causing acute discomfort for all of the adults—especially the grandparents—and a stress-loaded, tension-packed atmosphere whenever the families got together. The eighteen-month-old child continued to wet the bed intermittently, usually following extended visits filled with conflict with his cousins, until he was twelve years old. The unrestricted conflict between the children, *which was never discussed in the open,* continued unabated for years, giving rise to acrimony, hard feelings, gossip, slander, as well as acute childhood and adult stress. To this day, over twenty years later, the cousins do not associate with one another, aunts and uncles are not respected, and the sporadic and forced family get-togethers are tense, unhappy experiences. Why? Because cowardly adults acted irresponsibly.

Popular secular opinion says that conflict is natural. True. It is natural. But not spiritual. Many adults advocate letting children "solve their own conflicts"; some would even deliberately ignore physical conflict as long as it does not reach "harmful" or "dangerous" levels. Many secular experts encourage allowing children to "settle their own differences." However, any advice that allows reasoned differences of opinion such as arguments to proceed to quarreling or other evidence of a loss of control should be rejected. Scripture is very clear on how adults, and children, are to resolve differences (Matthew 18:15-17; Romans 12:9-10; I Timothy 5:21). And the methods in God's Word do not include "fighting it out." Where children are allowed to follow their baser instincts, acute stress will always follow.

More significant, though, than quarreling with peers is the acute stress children experience when they observe unloving behavior in the form of sarcasm, ridicule, neglect, pouting, and "the silent treatment" on the part of the significant adults in their life. Next to the actual trauma of death or divorce is the stress and anxiety a child experiences in anticipating that bitter adult conflict might lead to abandonment. Indeed, for many children, the prolonged stress of observing continuing parental conflict and the accompanying fear of the unknown, is more intense than the stress of actual separation itself.

Telling parents not to argue is unrealistic. All couples have their differences, and there is certainly room for private expressions of disagreement. *Admonishing parents not to quarrel,* however, is quite a different matter. One college student established the stress difference of each of these terms in these words.

> I can remember my parents arguing about stuff like where to go on vacation, or whether to buy this or that, or over some dumb things that we kids thought were stupid. Dad's habit of watching the weather report on three channels in a row is an example. But I can never remember an argument that made me think they didn't love each other. I even saw some arguments that verged on the petty bickering of a quarrel level, but shortly thereafter they were always normal, as usual. I don't remember that I was stressed out.

Contrast that memory with the statement of another student who confided:

> One time my parents didn't speak to each other for forty-three consecutive days. One of them tried, but the other just walked around in a deep silence. They would talk to us kids, but not to each other. It was

incredible. I felt like one of those hostages in
a movie. You know, their captor straps
dynamite on them and threatens to pull the
pin. I was so scared, but I can't tell you to
this day what I was scared of.

We ignore, at our children's peril, Biblical resolution
of our differences. A part of the problem is blind adherence
to the opinions of humanistic experts.

Step 5. *Give children responsibility.*

Current research in stress management indicates that
important factors in managing stress include a sense of
control, a sense of commitment to something, and the
quality of "character." One way to provide these factors in
the home is to assign definite tasks to children, tasks that
they can do which are appropriate for their age. These
include setting the table, doing dishes, general clean-up
chores, and similar activities.

For some reason, maybe because they've ignored the
Bible, modern parents almost universally fear demanding too
much of their children; consequently, many children do
nothing at all. Examples abound of teenagers who eat, sleep,
enjoy school and recreation, but do nothing at all at home.
Parents or other adults prepare meals, serve, and do dishes,
while children assume no responsibility whatsoever. They
develop no sense of self-worth. They develop no character,
no sensitivity to others, and no sense of control. The adults
are in charge. They are responsible.

However, stress is sure to ensue as a result since, sooner
or later, the parents will vent their frustration:

- on each other;
- on the children, through a direct reprimand
  related to the children's laziness (which, by the
  way, will go unheeded);

- on the children, through non-verbal negative communication;
- on the children, through nagging, sarcasm, or ridicule;
- on the children, but in connection with some unrelated incident that allows parents to vent their accumulated tensions.

Everyone is stressed because children are not given responsibility and because parents are fearful of overburdening children loaded down with homework, sports, and social demands. Through the years I have taught over ten thousand students at all levels. The most well-adjusted, stress-resistant young people I have met have been young people who had realistic and reasonable responsibilities at home.

But there is a fine line between realistic and unreasonable. Too many elementary school age children—nine, ten, and eleven year olds—are forced to care for younger siblings at home and "front" for irresponsible parents when the social worker comes to the door. Too much responsibility is not good. Too little responsibility is equally a stress producer. But you, a Christian parent, are the best judge of your child's ability to handle responsibility. If you care enough to read this book, you have obviously done other prayerful thinking about raising your child so that he, like the twelve-year-old Jesus, will "grow in wisdom, and stature, and in favor with God and man."

You are the expert on your child. Assert your expertise without hesitation. One more example may indelibly establish this point.

One very mature young woman shared with a group of young people the fact that in her home there were no secrets. "Of course," she laughed, "surprises were kept a secret, but my parents never allowed my brother, sister, or me to whisper a 'secret' about anyone or anything that could make anyone else in the family feel excluded. Nor did they allow us to tease, ridicule, or fight. We had first claim on certain things that were 'ours,' things we didn't have to share involuntarily, but we learned to respect one another's dignity. As far back as I can remember, we had to knock when we encountered a closed door in our house; we had to respect one another's privacy; we were never allowed to interrupt, and if we had a complaint about a family member, that person had to be there when we expressed it. I never had the insecurity or stress of enduring a negative 'whisper' about me, or of wondering what was said about me. If I wasn't allowed to gossip about anyone else, neither could anyone else gossip about me."

Step 6. *Control the environment.*

It almost goes without saying that much childhood stress is imposed upon children by unsuitable stimuli introduced into the home by outside sources including school, social organizations, radio, television, and, yes, even church-related organizations. There is an "off" switch or a "volume con-trol" switch available to every parent for each one of these stimuli. Monitor your child. Watch for signs of stress and inappropriate responses to it. Evaluate the source of the stress. Then use the "off" switch or the "volume" control. "Volume," in this case, means "how much," and reduces the stress stimuli. Remember: *You* are your child's first line of defense against stress.

Questions for Parents

1. Share a memory from your childhood which either increased your feeling of security or detracted from it.

2. What specific things can you do to help your child feel secure?

3. How does your faith in Christ shape your feelings of security? How should your faith affect your children's feelings of security?

4. What specific things can you do to enhance interpersonal relationships within your immediate family, your extended family, and your friends?

5. Write out your philosophy of discipline and an effective plan for consistent, loving expression of it with your children.

6. Examine your relationship with your spouse and/or your children in light of Step 4. What can you do to enhance your patterns of communication?

Questions for Children and Parents

1. If your children have accepted Christ as Savior, have them recount that experience. If they have not, share your testimony. Then, discuss how faith in Christ helps one to feel more secure.

2. Ask your children what specific things or people make them feel insecure. You might refer to the list of "Causes of Stress in the Home."

3. Discuss discipline with your children. Ask them how they think they should be punished for specific infractions of family rules. Ask them, if they are old enough, for rules they feel would be fair. Follow Step 2, and let them know what you expect and what the consequences of disobedience are.

4. If you have not already done so, outline specific areas of responsibility for each child. Explain the reasons or need for this responsibility as well as the consequences of not completing it.

[1] It is worth mentioning here, even though space does not permit a full discussion, that diet has been shown to be directly related to some behavior and emotional problems, including anxiety and stress in children. Parents who have no logical explanation for aberrant behavior or anxiety on the part of their children, should consider, with a physician, the possible impact of diet. (Susan

Smelzer, "Nutrition and Educational Performance," unpublished research paper for Dr. A. Burron, March 1986, University of Northern Colorado.)

CHAPTER FIVE

Reducing Stress
at School

HOW WOULD YOU REACT IF you had a job that you couldn't quit, and each day, day in and day out, you were forced to face the stress of:

1. A boss who ignores your feelings and ideas and constantly shows favor to your co-workers, or, worse yet, who continually criticizes you, assigns distasteful tasks to you, belittles you, or otherwise causes you mental, emotional, physical, and social distress.

2. Having to work at tasks that are too hard for you, so that you often receive reprimands for not doing the job right or for not finishing the job.

3. Having to work at a task too easy for you, so that you often receive reprimands for loafing or you feel bored, frustrated, and trapped.

4. Finding yourself placed in a group of co-workers who, like you, are looked down upon by the boss and by other workers as being unprepared, "dumb," incompetent, or otherwise abnormal or below average.

5. Being deprived of your "break" periods because you do not complete your work or because you did not do it according to the boss's expectations.

6. Having to take work home, night after night, often

facing the additional problems of being overtired, having other work to do, having no place to do the work, not knowing exactly what to do, or how to do it, and fearing the consequences of not meeting the boss's expectations the next morning.

7. Being pressured by everyone at home to advance faster in the company, to get a raise in salary, to get higher achievement ratings or other rewards.

8. Being ignored, excluded, and ostracized by your co-workers; being left out of social activities; being last on the list of those chosen to be a part of company teams; or being mocked because of your shape, your size, your appearance, your value system, or some other factor you can do little or nothing to change.

9. Being physically bullied by aggressive co-workers or by people from other companies in the neighborhood, to the point that you suffer physical assault on a regular basis.

10. Having to ride the company bus or van for extended periods of time both to and from work, oftentimes being verbally or physically assaulted on the bus.

11. Having your personal possession stolen from your worktable; being accused and judged guilty of a breach of company policy or social mores without having a fair chance to defend yourself.

12. Being regarded as inconsequential or valueless to company recreational teams, even though you try your best; and, since the focus is supposed to be fun, not going to any lengths to win, and being criticized for it.

13. Having to make up work you missed during an illness or family emergency, in addition to doing your normal amount of work.

14. Being indirectly, but pointedly, pressured to work harder and to achieve more, either by favorable or unfavorable comparison with relatives or friends.

15. Having your basic belief system matter-of-factly and

systematically criticized, directly or indirectly, by co-workers, the boss, outside consultants, and/or the president of the company.

If all of these stress occurred on your job, life would be extremely difficult, to say the least. You would need all the encouragement you could get, and if you knew some influential shareholders in the company, you would undoubtedly ask their help. Or—if you felt the situation was hopeless—you would find some way to quit.

The stresses identified in your hypothetical job *are stresses faced by today's children in every public school in the country.* Undeniably, some schools are better than others. It is also true that not all children face all of the stresses described above. But equally undeniable and true is the fact that all children will eventually face some of these stresses at school. What is of extreme importance, though, is that, with appropriate action from parents and educators, none of these stresses need be imposed on our children. If you really want to, you can make a difference.

Let's examine the list of job stresses and their parallels in school. At the same time, let's look at what we can do to help our children avoid unnecessary stress and to help them manage the school stresses that we, as responsible and caring parents, are unable to weed out.

WHAT WE CAN DO ABOUT STRESSES

The hypothetical job stresses and their parallels for children in school are amazingly similar, including the fact that—until age sixteen—children can't just "quit." However, if we fail to protect them as we should, they will find other ways to quit including "acting out," feigning repeated illness, becoming ill with real maladies, substance abuse, and a host of other avenues of relief. (See chapter 3.) But let's analyze this critical area of potential stresses.

Job Problem 1:	*An insensitive or emotionally troubled boss; a boss unfit for the job; an unprincipled boss.*
School Parallel 1:	*A teacher who plays favorites; who picks on certain children; who uses shame, embarrassment or other inappropriate interactive techniques.*

Any type of continuing personality conflict between child and teacher can be *extremely* stressful, and should not be allowed to continue. Consider just two examples from a large urban school district. A fifth grade teacher was charged with shoving a student into a trash can. Another teacher was the object of dismissal proceedings for forcing a student to bite a bar of soap. Both of these instances occurred within the space of a few weeks. According to the Associated Press, one teacher decided to paddle at least twenty-five students in what the AP termed a "day of reckoning" at the end of the year. The teacher, instead of paddling students when improper behavior took place, "saved up" the spankings until the end of the academic year in June.1 Imagine the stress some students faced in expectation of deferred, but inevitable, physical and emotional punishment.

Job Problem 2 and 3:	*Tasks too hard, reprimands, un-finished work.* *Tasks too easy, reprimands, bore-dom and frustration.*

School Parallel 2 and 3:   *The child is misdiagnosed or misplaced in a learning group or into certain materials.*

A common problem? Yes. In 1987, the Denver Public Schools admitted to having erred in diagnosing and placing hundreds of students. The result? Potentially severe stress to the students. In Pueblo, Colorado, a high school student was reported to have been considered mentally retarded, even though he successfully managed a service station after school, including handling the bank deposits. Children are often misdiagnosed and assigned work that is inappropriate. The result: Stress, sometimes acute and prolonged stress.

Job Problem 4:   *Enduring the stigma of being labeled or otherwise regarded as inferior.*

School Parallel 4:   *Being placed with the slow group, or otherwise being identified as an underachiever; suffering the stress of being stigmatized.*

An extreme example of both parent and child stress resulting from such a situation was reported by the Associated Press in June of 1984, in Henryetta, Oklahoma:

HENRYETTA, Okla. (AP)—A first-grade teacher has flunked all 15 students in her class, saying they were immature and "just not ready for the second grade."

The mass flunking has prompted protests from parents, some of whom are threatening to take their children out of the schools in this east-central Oklahoma town of 7,000.

The first grade in the school district is divided into several levels, depending on assessments of the students' maturity and abilities, Duncan told the Tulsa World.

Duncan said the 15 children were held back because of "immaturity and their lack of ability to sit still because of their short attention span."

She said the children did improve during the year, but were "just not ready for the second grade."

Samuel and Patty Gray plan to transfer their son, Eric, to another school district where they were assured he could start the second grade, the newspaper said.

"Eric's just an average 6-year-old. He likes to play, and if he's bored his attention will wander," Gray said. "But his work was satisfactory. . . ."[2]

Research has indicated that pupils tend to live up—or down—to expectations of them. Being held back, or flunked, is stressful for a child. It is a stress which need not be, and should not be, imposed upon a child, as we shall see later in this chapter. But it can usually be avoided only if we act as our child's first line of defense against stress.

Job Stress 5 and 6: *Missing break periods; taking loads of work home.*

School Parallel 5 and 6: *Missing recess or other privileges because of failure to complete seatwork or*

*homework consistent
with the teacher's
expectations;
having to take work
home which
you may not
understand, which
you might not have
time to do because of
family, church or
other obligations,
or for which you do
not have a place
to work.*

Other problems pointing to the stress of homework can be described, but one point emerges with clarity:

Homework can often interfere with activities
which are far more beneficial to the child
than extended schoolwork. Homework has
been insisted upon by parents in many cases
to teach children responsibility or to keep
them off the streets. Yet the teaching of
responsibility, while it can be a legitimate
function of the schools, is primarily a
function of the home. Keeping children
productively engaged is also the responsibility
of the home. It is not the responsibility of the
school to control the hordes of kids
wandering around shopping malls or hanging
around video arcades. If parents uncritically
demand more and more homework, the end
result will be the extension of the tentacles of
the public school in every area of parental

responsibility. The home will be invaded and spiritual development will be pushed aside.

Numerous other facts challenge the desirability of increased homework. The demands upon a child's time are often incredible. He may need to be at the school bus stop by 7:00 a.m. He may ride a school bus for an hour. His whole day may be occupied with classes and with extracurricular activities. He may not arrive home until 6:00 p.m., at which time he may have music lessons, assignments from church, or a part-time job. He should also have home chores to do.

If parents demand more homework and pile other responsibilities upon a child who is already overloaded and who does not have the opportunity for quiet moments of reflection, personal devotion or meditation, or a quiet, peaceful dialogue with mother and father, the parents indeed "know not what they do."

Another factor to consider is that not all children have a quiet area at home in which to study, or parents to help them. On the contrary, some parental attempts to help may degenerate into tension-filled parent/child conflict. Where there is no place to work, children may end up failing because they are circumstantially, rather than academically, unable to keep up.[3]

Job Stress 7:

Facing the pressure of performance stress, the stress of constant high achievement, of winning, of being first, of succeeding, of being advanced or on an accelerated career track.

School Parallel 7 and 14:

Parental pressure for good grades, for making the varsity, for landing the lead in the school play, for being first violin, or otherwise outdoing others by competing with them and defeating them; stress imposed by being encouraged to be more like a favored brother or sister.

For children whose disposition is non-competitive, easygoing, and oriented toward "doing my best," parental pressure of a more competitive emphasis can be extremely stressful. Many well-meaning parents end up creating a situation similar to the life story of Jimmy Piersall, a major league baseball player who experienced the terror of mental illness. During a verbal confrontation in a mental institution, he shouted, "Leave my father out of this. If it hadn't been for my father, I wouldn't be where I am today!" In that moment, he realized exactly where he was, and the real significance of what he had just said. Parental pressure for "success," resulted in acute distress, a fact which, unfortunately, still escapes many parents today.

Job Stress 8,9,10, and 11:

Suffering the stress of being ostracized, excluded, belittled, assaulted, or otherwise subjected to gross indignity by co-workers either on the job, at social functions, or on the way to work.

School Parallel 8,9,10, and 11:

The parallels here are obvious. It is common for children to suffer the stresses of:
• peer pressure, taunting, and being socially ignored or tormented;
• being beaten or pushed around by bullies;
• being terrorized on the school bus;
• having one's

belongings stolen. In this latter case, children often suffer the additional stress of seeing the thief with the stolen item but being unable to prove their ownership or the fact that the item was stolen. They may even be threatened with harm if the theft is reported.

I believe that the stress of peer pressure is one of the most severe and most difficult to manage by children. It is also one of the most difficult for parents to alleviate. Parents can take steps to halt physical abuse or fighting, but emotional abuse in the form of being left out, teased, taunted, ridiculed, or humiliated is almost impossible for a parent to successfully step in and stop.

Many examples show that peer pressure and the necessity for a good self-image can lead to acute stress and acute reactions to stress.

I can't stand another day of school, and especially another minute without television. Please tell my classmates what happened and watch if they are sad or if they laugh. But that's obvious. I never really had any friends.[4]

These were the last words of an unhappy, overweight sixteen-year-old, scribbled in a suicide note left for his parents in Oakley, California. The despondent youngster, whose days at school were filled with misery, perceived himself to be totally unpopular—and, hence, worthless—as a result of being fat and unattractive. He had found only one source of peace of mind: television. When his parents took away his television set to discipline him for feigning sickness in order to cut school, the stress was too much for him. The secure world of his room and his television set had become the only place he could function, with some degree of control, without worrying about being rejected. He could not face the stress of school, and now he could not face the stress of life out of school. He had no reserves to draw upon. To him, death was his only escape.

> In a suburb of Dallas, Texas, a fourteen-year-old boy described by his parents as a happy child, shot and killed himself with a .357 Magnum pistol after returning from a trip to a dentist. No note was found. There was only one clue as to why the boy might have killed himself. He had come home from the dentist's office with a mouthful of braces. The underlying reason for his suicide was the same reason that motivated the suicide of the overweight teenager in California.[5]

> In Manchester, Missouri, another fourteen-year-old's collapse under the same stress took a form similar to that of the fourteen-year-old in the Dallas suburb. Bursting into a junior high school study hall, the boy shouted, "I can't stand it anymore! Now everybody shut up!" He then bellowed at an adversary in the study hall, "You won't call my brother a _____ anymore," and fatally shot him.[5]

What the boy could not stand, the Associated Press reported was continued taunting about his family by his junior high school classmates. The stress had become too much for him to take. Described as a "nice boy who had won a good citizenship award" prior to his emotional collapse and who had also been called "an above average student" by the school principal, the tormented adolescent began his rampage by firing shots from a .22 caliber pistol into the ceiling of the gymnasium of his junior high school.

Each of the above cases represents the most extreme result of young peoples' inability to cope with the stress of peer pressure. Yet the problem of peer pressure is something few adults fully appreciate. Most adults, who are themselves striving to cope with the stresses of paying bills, making ends meet, satisfying the boss, meeting quotas, surviving rush hour traffic, and dealing with their own interpersonal crises hardly ever give peer pressure a thought.

One of the sources of escape from stressful situations for many adults is to flee mentally into the solace of the past, into the carefree world of childhood, where happy times are fondly remembered and where an unawareness of problems was virtually nonexistent.

When adults delve into the past and begin to rummage among their memories, many unpleasant and unhappy events are remembered. Undoubtedly, among those most painful events, are situations in which the source of the pain was the same source leading to the unhappiness and misery of each of the teenagers in the tragedies described above: The stress of rejection.

Unlike adults, who bring a sophisticated array of psychological defense mechanisms to situations in which rejection is encountered, children do not have well-defined defense mechanisms. They are, therefore, particularly vulnerable to the stress of rejection. This fear of rejection was documented in a 1986 survey of several thousand pre-adolescents who ranked "fear of saying the wrong thing" as a significant source of anxiety.

Professionals in the field of education and psychology have recognized for decades the tremendous impact that peer pressure and acceptance or rejection by their peer group can have on young people. If children are not carefully taught throughout their developmental process to recognize and evaluate peer pressure in both its overt and more subtle forms, children will succumb to such pressure. Several negative results can occur from that. Children—and even young adults—may accommodate themselves to the values of the peer group in order to gain or maintain acceptance. If they fail to gain acceptance by the peer group, they will employ various defense mechanisms or seek various avenues of escape from the fact of their rejection. Some methods of seeking escape from the stress of rejection have positive results. Children compensate by becoming superior in some area of achievement. More often, however, the method of escape is destructive to the child's emotional, spiritual, and even physical development.

Although the pain of rejection by the peer group is perhaps the most acute form of rejection a child can experience, other forms of rejection also impose serious amounts of emotional stress upon children. For example, it is an extremely painful experience to be rejected by being cut from an athletic team or passed over for a part in a play; or, by being forced to sit on the sidelines as a substitute; or, to fail to compete successfully even in situations where winning could not be conceivably significant. Rejection by people called significant others, such as older brothers or sisters, admired relatives, or even a parent can constitute a serious form of stress upon a child. But rejection as a source of stress goes even further than an actual painful experience. Rejection need not be real to cause stress. Rejection may be only perceived or anticipated, yet perceived or anticipated rejection is as real as the actual occurrence to a child.

Job Stress 12:

Being regarded as valueless or inconsequential to a group effort by your co-workers and department, despite being a hard worker and an eager participant.

School Parallel 12:

Being a "bench sitter" on a school team, an understudy in a school play, or being "cut" entirely from participation in extra-curricular activities because you are deemed "not good enough."

Any adult who has ever experienced being the last player chosen, or any of the above situations, can probably still feel the sting of the experience. No further proof that such school experiences are stressful is necessary.

Job Stress 15:

Having to hide or constantly defend one's fundamental beliefs or values because of mockery or ridicule by co-workers.

School Parallel 15:

Open challenges by teachers and/or other students who are totally opposed to your child's religious or moral beliefs, constant indoctrination in humanistic values, or insidious threats because of nonconformity to general value systems.

One example is that of creationists who work in public education. Many times they are ridiculed for their "unscientific" beliefs. Christians in other "progressive" fields are frequently laughed at by co-workers for things such as prayer, church attendance, and witnessing. For many adults, the stress of finding their belief system under constant attack is severe whether at work or in society in general.

For a child, the constant barrage of instruction and values which are totally opposed to the values of their Christian home can be devastating, or certainly confusing. Parents who seek to influence textbook selection are often attacked as rednecked censors. In another example in one suburban school district, sixth grade students were forced to listen to a homosexual male defend the legitimacy of his "alternative lifestyle." When the parents protested, they were ridiculed as "fundamentalist fanatics." These types of situations create stress for both students and parents.

WHAT TO DO ABOUT SCHOOL STRESS

Although many of the stresses faced by children in public schools are commonly encountered, or not unusual, *that does not mean that they are necessary*. Nor does it mean that they should be tolerated by responsible parents, Christian or non-Christian. Not one of these stresses is necessary. Not one of these stresses is educationally justifiable. Not one of these stresses is unavoidable.

In the previously mentioned book, Classrooms in Crisis, detailed strategies on how to initiate contact with the school, how to build a defensible case, how to have measurable impact on school curriculum, and how to initiate other major educational policy-shaping procedures are presented. It is recommended that concerned parents arm themselves with the information in that book. In addition to the major efforts outlined in *Classrooms in Crisis,* the following facts and actions can be utilized in helping children manage school stress.

FACTS AND ACTIONS TO AVOID OR MANAGE SCHOOL STRESS

We are now at what can be the "easy" part of helping your child manage school stress. Whether the task is easy or hard is up to you. The actual actions to initiate are not difficult. The difficulty lies in shaking off some of our fears and attitudes regarding our own stress level, in being assertive, and in exercising our rights and responsibilities as parents. It is not easy to enter a foreign environment such as the school and to assert our rights and our child's rights with professionals who "know best." Nevertheless, the stress for us as adults will be easier to manage than the stresses our children might have to face if we abdicate our responsibilities. Even parents who are also teachers do not particularly enjoy taking the initiatives below. It is also true that, all things considered, we would rather ignore potential or actual problems and maybe just "pray them away."

However, after admitted to all of our stresses, let's do as Nehemiah did when he was charged with the task of rebuilding the walls of Jerusalem in the face of an imminent attack by hostile forces. "But we prayed to our God, and because of them [our enemies] we set up a guard against them day and night" (Nehemiah 4:9). In other words, we must pray because everything depends on God, but we must work as though everything depends on us. Take the initiative. You can reduce your children's stress.

Initiative 1

As a professional educator with over a quarter of a century of experience, I am convinced that the single, most important factor in a child's education is the belief system and the personality of his teacher. It is far more important than the teacher's education, the physical environment of the school, the quality of the materials, the social structure of the classroom, or any other education-oriented factor. This does not mean, of course, that other factors are not important; obviously, a delightfully gregarious illiterate holding classes on penmanship out on the open range of the windswept plains near Douglas, Wyoming, would not be a wise choice as a reading teacher for a first grader. It does mean, though, that parents should be *vitally* concerned, first and foremost, with knowing the kind of person an *otherwise qualified* person is. Then, the following steps can be taken to help our children avoid and manage the stresses described in the "School Parallels" section, above.

1. Some districts have open enrollment. This allows parents to enroll children in a school or a classroom of their choice. Exercise the option. It is worth the cost of any inconvenience. Visit schools, talk to teachers, and select your child's teacher carefully, if possible. At the secondary level, you can request specific teachers for specific subjects.

2. Where open enrollment is not an option but where there is more than one classroom per grade, it is usually possible to have your reasonable request honored for assignment of your child to a specific teacher.

3. Where no choices are available, plan to be a frequent and friendly visitor to your child's classroom. Visit the classroom before your child attends. Talk to the teacher.[6] Volunteer for classroom or school tasks, such as room mother or teacher's aide in elementary grades, or as a chaperone or parent-helper at social or athletic functions for junior-high or high-school students. Remember, though, that teachers can be stressed by a threatening parent or by what they interpret as a parental threat. Emphasize the fact that you and the teacher are partners.

4. Have an impact on classroom and school policy. Some specific steps on how to have influence in your child's school are:

    a. *Seek change, not catharsis.* When you approach a teacher, principal, or a problem, be specific. Do not ask "non-questions" or make vague accusations. Work with your child's teachers and administrators.

    b. *Never forget that teachers are people, too.* They have the same anxieties, fears, hopes, and desires you do. Recognize the teacher's needs: for recognition, to do a good job, to be treated fairly, to feel secure in his position. Approach every situation with love and respect. "Therefore however you want people to treat you, so treat them" (Matthew 7:12). Successful positive communication begins with sensitivity and a rejection of an adversarial relationship.

    c. *Commend or criticize with impact.* There are specific ways to do this. If you are commending the teacher, put it in writing. Address the letter to the principal and copy it to the teacher. If you

97

have a complaint, the scriptural pattern for resolving conflicts among believers would also apply here. Go to the teacher privately first to resolve it (Matthew 18:15). If that fails, take along another parent who shares your concern—as an observer, not another accuser. Only if that fails should you write to the principal. If this is necessary, be specific. Document your previous efforts to resolve the situation with the teacher and ask for specific actions. Send a copy of that letter to the teacher also.

d. *Do your homework.* Read and understand the school district's rules, your child's classroom rules, and the school's rules. If your child's school has forms which must be completed regarding curriculum content or methodology questions, know what they are and file them with the proper persons. Know your school district's policy on selecting materials, teachers, and activities.

e. *Influence your schools by influencing the community.* If parents organize for action, school administrators will listen. Also, remember that public school administrators are sensitive to the voters who control their financial base.

f. *Become a decision maker in your child's school.* Some school districts have formal statements explaining how parents can become involved in committees and organizations. Find out if there is a School Accountability Council, Materials Selection Committee, Teacher Evaluation Committee, Teacher Selection Committee, or a Parents' Advisory Council.

Most public school administrators welcome parental input because that frequently translates into greater parental involvement, better working conditions, higher salaries, better morale, and more support. Vague, strident complaints or threats will be self-defeating. If you truly want to alleviate your stress over specific situations or your child's stress, these suggestions will help. For more complete details, I would highly recommend the book Classrooms in Crisis, chapter 8.

Initiatives 2,3,4

Ask your child's prospective principal or teacher how children are grouped, tracked, or otherwise placed into learning experiences. You can help your child avoid the stresses identified in School Parallels 2 and 3 if you let school personnel know that you expect *different grouping standards for different subjects.*

For example, a reading test score is not the best criterion for grouping children for math instruction or for physical education. Children should not be placed in the "average," "slow," or "fast" group for every subject, unless it can be demonstrated that there is a good reason for such placement. Thus, if a teacher says, "We use a book in science class. Your child is in the low category in reading, so he's in the low science group." Then, if you discover that science class is mostly audiovisual experiences, field trips, discussions, and experiments, you should assertively questions whether your child is receiving instruction appropriate for his abilities in science.

Remember the example of the teacher who "flunked" all of her students? Today's teachers are taught to *individualize* instruction for children. This means that children have a program laid out for them that is based upon their individual abilities. They're not "flunked" according to some external standard and then retaught the same content with the possibility that they will fail again. Imagine the stress of a thirteen-year-old third grader, a giant among his or her eight-year-old classmates, who has failed the external standards.

Ask about your school's attitude toward grouping and individualization. Express your belief that children should receive individualized instruction. Assert your desire not to have your child stigmatized if he is not accelerated in one or more areas or pressured in all areas if he is advanced in only one or two subjects. If necessary, take a professional educator along. Many teachers are fighting against district-imposed "lock-step" courses of study and will willingly help parents fight for individualized programs.

For example, the average shoe size of sixth graders is a size six. What would be the reaction of school administrators and parents if the physical education teacher established three groups on the bases of shoe size: accelerated, sizes seven and eight; average, size six; and below average, sizes four and five? Shoes must be individually sized. So must a school's entire educational program.

Children do not all fit into one mold. Programs, expectations, and materials must be individualized to bring out the best in each child. Many childhood stresses, ranging from emotional to academic, can be avoided if you encourage your child's school officials to pursue sound educational practices.

Initiative 5

Many stresses imposed upon children at school have their origins in the unreasonable expectations of well-intentioned parents. (See School Stress 12.) It is not uncommon to have school programs for the gifted flooded with applications from parents whose children lack, not only the academic gifts, but also the desire to participate in such programs. Many parents have pressured teachers into placing children into learning groups with materials that are too advanced for them. It is no accident that requests for placement into lower groups or easier materials are almost non-existent. Pride is never a godly virtue. First John 2:16 tells us it is a worldly emotion. Yet it motivates parents to use their children's achievements as personal trophies in a never-ending quest for recognition. Parent-induced stress is one of the most severe stresses upon children.

Parental demands are also the source of one of the major causes of school stress for children: homework. This problem has been discussed earlier in this chapter. At this point let's look at some solutions to the problem.

Before demanding more homework, concerned parents should know:

a) What kind of homework you want;

b) How much homework you want:

c) The reasons why you want homework.

> Not all homework is valuable. Indeed, homework may be detrimental to the very values, attitudes and behaviors you, as a Christian parent, want to develop in your children.

> The most defensible homework for those whose primary concern is the development of spirituality and personal responsibility is precisely that, home work: helping one's parents meet the responsibilities and challenges of day-to-day living in contemporary society; addressing the needs of grandparents and relatives; helping neighbors; working at part-time jobs; and doing chores.

> As a Christian, you have the right to influence the education of your child by demanding only quality school assignments so that the full influence of the church can be felt by your child and your family. Influence the education of your child by reserving to yourself the prerogative of selecting some of your child's educational activities from community

agencies, church groups, community colleges, community recreational organizations and private agencies. Influence your child's education by carefully considering the many opportunities which exist beyond the confines of the school classroom and beyond the influence of a few educators who may not share your perspective of what constitutes valuable knowledge. Influence your schools by demanding very clearly outlined policies on extracurricular activities, including clear-cut policies on the nature, the extent, and the scope of homework assignments.[7]

It is also only through the influence of parents that the "winning at all costs"—or *performance stress* emphasis in the public schools can be reduced. Performance stress is experienced by children as young as four years old, and it occurs when children are placed into competition of any sort— artistic, musical, athletic, academic—where the emphasis is placed upon winning trophies, prizes, accolades, honors, or other recognition, rather than upon doing one's bet with the abilities God has given. Stress is created for children who:

- are forced to "sit the bench";
- fail to make the team, the cast, the choir, or other group— especially after public try-outs;
- are publicly or privately berated for not performing at a level yielding a victory or an accolade;
- must contemplate making a mistake and being publicly humiliated;
- actually make an error or a mistake—again, in public, before their peers or adults;
- undergo intensive, prolonged, emotion-filled practice sessions;
- face the time stress of scheduling homework, practices, performances, and other demands.

I have counseled many parents and participants for whom performance stress, fueled by the "winning is the only thing that counts" mentality, became unbearable, including situations in which:

- A nineteen-year-old male athlete, a member of high school's starting basketball team, sobbed uncontrollably after his team won the state championship. He had been "benched" at the end of the first half after making a mistake, and he suffered his humiliation in front of parents, grand-parents, and friends. Because his team was significantly ahead, his coach could afford to "make an example" of him.

- A fifteen-year-old performer, an understudy called upon to fill in for the lead in a school play, suffered repeated episodes of bed-wetting after being roundly criticized by her drama coach and the local newspaper drama editor. The latter flavored her review with the comment: "The lackluster performance of _____, under-study to _____, was only one of the reasons why the play didn't work." The student, four years later, will not participate in any way in a public forum.

- An eight-year-old, who had worked his heart out on a creative art project, totally abandoned his out-of-school creative art projects after his teacher publicly displayed only what she considered to be "the best" projects at parent teacher night. His painfully-achieved project was excluded.

- Yet another child, an eleven-year-old, displayed a

sudden rash of aggressive and defiant behavior. It was ultimately traced to the fact that he, along with only five of thirty other children, was not allowed to work on a class mural because, "it will be hung in the hallway, and we want only our best work."

Not only is the "winning-is-everything" mentality extremely injurious to children, not only is it *totally unnecessary, not only is it in violation of stated school policy in many districts, it is also totally unscriptural. It is guaranteed to produce stress in any child whose parents allow him to place value on being "first" by comparing himself with others, rather than by valuing himself according to God's Word.* Consider these Scriptures: I Timothy 5:21; Ephesians 6:3-4; Romans 12:10; Galatians 5:26, 6:4.

It is important to cultivate in children the attitude that, "if I seek to do my best and to honor God with my efforts, then He will bless my efforts according to His will. I have an internal, God-sanctified, standard of evaluation, so that whatever I do 'in word or deed, do all in the name of the Lord Jesus, giving thanks through Him to God the Father'" (Colossians 3:17).

I have had the experience of being a "winning" coach in several sports. Nevertheless, I am so convinced of the extremely stressful effects on children of an emphasis on "performance" rather than "participation," that I went to great lengths to repeatedly emphasize and discuss with my children the Scriptures outlined above. I tried to encourage and direct my children into individual endeavors and extracurricular activities sponsored by agencies whose goal was neither school nor team glory, nor career enhancement of adult leaders.

The negative aspects of performance stress can be avoided and the positive aspects of the excitement of participation and competition can be emphasized if parents will take an active role in guiding their children. Some parents encourage their children to pursue activities that focus upon individual effort and training: bodybuilding, cycling, weight lifting, tennis, skiing, golf, track and field, art lessons, music lessons, hiking, fishing, crafts, and other enrichment activities. Some parents reduce stress by being a constant source of influence upon the attitudes of school personnel and upon the philosophy of extracurricular school programs. And some, like the father and mother of the nineteen-year-old senior whose muffled sobs belied the victory celebration of the state basketball champs, will write letters to the editor, appear on talk radio shows, and otherwise challenge a destructive trend in the public schools. Still other parents will do "all of the above," bearing in mind the ultimate goal of stress reduction for their children—faith in Jesus Christ as Savior and an attitude of humbling oneself to serve others.

Initiative 6

Combating the stress of School Parallels 8,9,10, and 11 is a step many parents hesitate to take for fear of interfering, or, in some cases, because their children mistakenly beg parents not to interfere. They are afraid of further ridicule or taunting by the peer group.

What would you do in this case?

> Nine-year-old Jennifer was inconsolable.
> Her emotions were so intense that she
> couldn't possibly have hidden them.
> During quiet-time at school that day, the
> teacher had allowed Sally, a classmate, to
> distribute invitations to her birthday
> party. Up and down the rows went Sally,
> proudly distributing the coveted

invitations, pointedly excluding Jennifer and two other children. The teacher, busy with a bulletin board display, either didn't notice, or the callous disregard of Jennifer's feelings and the feelings of the other two excluded children just didn't register. In either case, Jennifer's emotional stress was extreme—no amount of support from mom and dad was effective in repairing her battered self-esteem.

What would you do?

Jennifer's mother, overcoming her own stress, contacted the teacher and personally shared with the teacher her concern about her daughter's feelings. Fortunately, in this case, the teacher was a caring person, and she immediately called Sally's mother and expressed her concern about the "accidental" exclusion, the "oversight," which resulted in emotional anguish for three of her pupils. Unfortunately, Sally's mother was not guilty of an oversight. She made no bones about telling the teacher that, in effect, she and not the teacher, would choose her child's friends, and that the exclusion was her prerogative because it was, in her opinion, "a free country!"

Jennifer did not get to go to the party. But thereafter, no children in the school were allowed to initiate a private social function through the public-school classroom unless *all* children were invited. Children do have a right to choose their own friends. They do not have a right to use the public school as an avenue to discriminate against or humiliate their classmates. It took the reaction of enlightened hindsight, rather than the pre-action of anticipatory foresight, but a stress-reducing school policy was born.

There are many other examples of appropriate parental interventions when children are emotionally or physically abused by a peer group. Indeed, they are far too numerous to include here. It is important to remember, though, that peer abuse is such a severe form of stress for a child that no lawful step is too extreme for a parent to take. This includes personal intervention with the child's teacher, the principal, in other school activities, with the parents of the abusive peer antagonists, or, if necessary, by contacting other government authorities and, in extreme cases, taking legal action. Parents should never be forced, as one parent was, to have their child instructed in the martial arts due to a school administration that insisted upon letting children "fight their own battles," including physical battles! The struggle against abusive peers is not the child's "own battle." Children should not be forced to defend themselves because of the unenlightened carnality and foolishness of adults who pass the disastrous results of their folly off on children under the guise of "professional expertise."

Do not be afraid that you will be fighting your child's battles. They are not *his* battles. They are *yours*. You are a family. Intervening against insurmountable stresses imposed by a hostile value system in not only your legitimate responsibility, but it can be a shining example of godly parenting to other parents whose own inhibiting stresses prevent them from following their God-given instincts.

CHOOSING YOUR CHILD'S SCHOOL

Besides the numerous steps that have been recommended to this point, other alternative solutions are available. They require a major commitment from parents, and they are not always available. Nevertheless, many parents have elected to avoid public school altogether, since they know that the public school cannot meet their goals for their children. They know that only by a rare, happy "accident" can the public schools establish a learning atmosphere and a curriculum that will allow their children to grown in their faith and in their knowledge of Jesus Christ. For this reason, they choose one of these alternatives:

- Home schooling
- Nondenominational Christian schooling,
- Denominational Christian schooling.

There are advantages and disadvantages to each of these alternatives, and we'll consider some of them here. It should be mentioned that I have taught in both public and private schools; I have trained teachers and parents to teach in each of the situations above, and I am totally committed to the primary goal described in chapter 2. It should also be mentioned that my wife and I sent our children to public school and that the children, who are now twenty-three, twenty-two, and eighteen, had mostly edifying experiences. They are also committed Christians. We would not, however, have sent them to public school without following, to the letter, the Scriptural guidelines outlined in chapter 6.

ADVANTAGES AND DISADVANTAGES OF ALTERNATIVE SCHOOLING

Marie S. is a parent who approached me at a Home School Conference, and, as soon as she was confident that she wasn't being observed, burst into tears. "I'm trying to be a committed Christian parent," she confessed, "but I am totally frustrated teaching at home. I do fine with my seven year old, but the thirteen year old won't cooperate; she's never motivated; she lets out these sighs whenever I want her to do anything, and she does sloppy work. It's a constant hassle. Her dad gets home, and we have these daily 'scenes,' and by the time we're finished, the evening is ruined for everyone" Further conversation revealed that Marie was unsure of what and how to teach and that she had nagging doubts about whether the children were going to be adequately prepared when they eventually had to compete academically. When I suggested to her that home schooling might not be the answer for her family, she straightened up and virtually beamed with relief. She had succumbed to peer pressure and was attempting to do something she was neither emotionally nor academically equipped to do. The advantages of home schooling are obvious in the personalized attention and instruction. But home schooling often places stress upon children because of:

- a lack of preparation or inclination on their parents' part,
- ill-chosen academic materials,
- limited opportunity for peer interaction,
- limited opportunity for academically enriching activities.

In a like manner, the advantages and disadvantages of nondenominational and denominational Christian schools can be compared.

ADVANTAGES OF EACH

1. Maximal parental input into:
   a. curriculum
   b. extra-curricular goals and activities,
   c. choice of teacher for their child (in some cases),
   d. open lines of communication,
   e. mutual commitment to the goal of Christian growth.
2. Ready access to visitation privileges.
3. Shared faith with teachers: Common problem-solving procedures, attitudes, and goals.
4. Common expectations for discipline, classroom demeanor, out-of-school behavior.

There are no serious disadvantages to either type of school other than, perhaps, the following:

Nondenominational

1. Biblical teachings at variance with the parents' doctrinal positions.
2. Expense. There is usually no supporting church body; hence, sometimes high tuition and other fees are imposed.
3. Unrealistic expectations by parents.
4. Use of the school as a "dumping ground" for problem children.
5. Spiritual arrogance on the part of children.
6. Unrealistically high expectations for pupil deportment.

Denominational

1. Cliquishness of families if the supporting church is small.
2. Reluctance of parents to intervene, due to peer pressure from other adults in the church.
3. Focus on academic superiority to public school system—loss of focus on spiritual purpose.
4. Limited exposure of children to conflicting belief systems.
5. Use of school as a "dumping ground" for problem pupils.
6. Feelings of spiritual superiority.
7. Unrealistically high expectations for pupil deportment.

A major childhood stress to be alert for is the use of guilt in church-related schools as a pupil management technique.

A second major source of stress is academic pressure. Private schools are under immense pressure to demonstrate academic excellence, partially because segments of the Christian community have been so vocal and liberal in their criticism of the public schools. More often than might be imagined, children in Christian schools suffer the imposition of "performance stress" in academics, and their teachers are harassed by well-meaning parents who abuse the bond of faith to impose their good intentions upon underpaid and unappreciated teachers.

When Christian schools lose sight of their primary objective and when they succumb to the temptation to evaluate their achievements against standards of the secular world and the public schools, they become sources of stress for children. It should be remembered, too, that all children are sinners, and the same negative behaviors that emerge in the public schools are often as bad, or worse, in Christian schools, a fact which can be readily and extensively documented.

In summary, I would recommend a good Christian school—one with faith-building as a focus—over a good public school. But I would recommend a good public school over a mediocre Christian school, if parents can follow the precepts in chapter 6:

Many extreme sources of stress faced by adults in the workplace are closely analogous to stresses faced by children in their "jobs" at school. In most instances, these sources of stress are completely unnecessary; parents can and *should* take steps to help their children avoid them or, at the very least, to effectively manage them. Using persuasion based upon informed knowledge, common sense, school policy, legal initiative, and scripturally-inspired wisdom, parents can take the initiative in being the "yeast" which leavens the whole "loaf," turning the public-school experience into wholesome fare which nourishes all of the children in our society.

Questions for Parents

1. Select one or two stresses from the list at the beginning of the chapter and analyze your child's specific stress as compared to yours at work. How is it similar/dissimilar?

2. What can you do to relieve your child's stress?

3. What do you think is your child's greatest fear/stress?

4. What is the belief system and personality of your child's teacher(s)?

   If you do not know, outline specific steps you can take to become acquainted.

5. In what ways may your child be suffering from the "success/win" mentality?

Questions for Children and Parents

1. With your child, discuss what he sees as his/her greatest fear or stress.

2. Ask what kinds of personal attitudes and ideas their teachers express as the reason for human life, success, and so on.

3. Discuss with your child Joshua 1:8. Analyze together the basis of success defined in that verse compared to the world's philosophy of how to succeed.

[1] The Greeley, Colorado, *Tribune*, Friday, June 29, 1984, p. A-11.

[2] See note 1.

[3] Arnold Burron, et. al., *Classrooms in Crisis: Parents' Rights and the Public School* (Accent Publications: Denver, Colo., © 1986), pp. 121-122.

[4] Greeley, Colorado, *Tribune*, February 11, 1983, p. A-11.

[5] Denver, Colorado, *Denver Post*, February 16, 1984, p. 15A

[6] Appendix A, at the end of this book, includes a series of questions used by the Aurora Public Schools (Denver), CO, one of Colorado's largest school districts, to interview prospective teachers on how they relate to students. The questions are excellent.

[7] See note 3.

CHAPTER SIX

Helping Children Manage the Stress of Adversity

THE SECRET:
PARENTS DRAW STRENGTH FROM DYING BOY, 10.
IN HEAVEN IT WILL END

So read the headlines of the lead story on page 1 of the Greeley, Colorado *Tribune,* Sunday, February 2, 1986. Ten-year-old Mark Alexander was dying. The newspaper story was the result of an invitation Mark had extended to *Tribune* reporter Mike Peters so that Mark could be interviewed about his terminal illness and comfort his friends. Peters quoted the ten-year-old cancer victim liberally throughout the feature interview.

> "I don't think about it very often anymore," Mark said in a quiet voice from the couch. "I know that in heaven there won't be any more pain, no more sadness or sickness. In heaven it will end. In the first few days after I learned I was gonna die, I was petrified. Now it's easier. I started to calm down after awhile because I knew that after I die, I'd be with Jesus. My family and relatives understand it

too, and that makes it easier for me."

Mark's parents, Charles and Debbie Alexander, who had fought their son's leukemia with him for almost a year, were also liberally quoted, and provided deep insight into how the family worked together to overcome the stress of Mark's adversity.

> "He told us he wants his classmates to know that they shouldn't give up when they have problems—that you should keep fighting. A Christian attitude has helped tremendously," Debbie said. "Belief is very important and Mark really feels it now."

Reporter Peters also observed the reaction of Mark's six-year-old brother, Michael, noting that even he "seemed to accept Mark's illness."

But the most poignant part of the interview was reported by Mark's parents, who recalled what their son had said during a conversation the preceding week:

> I could just die quick and easy in an accident, but there must be a reason for me to die this way. There must be a special reason in heaven.

One week following the interview, Mark died. This ten-year-old child, facing extreme stress, was able to manage his stress with such strength that he was an inspiration to his parents, his brother, his classmates, and teachers at the Christian school he attended. He had been taught what the Apostle Paul calls "The Secret."

> I know how to get along with humble means, and I also know how to live in prosperity; in

any and every circumstance I have learned the
secret of being filled and going hungry, both
of having abundance and suffering need. I can
do all things through Him who strengthens
me. (Philippians 4:12-13)

A little over a year later, on August 26, 1987, the
Greeley, Colorado, *Tribune* on page A-3 chronicled another
story of a child's courage in the face of death. This time the
story was about fourteen-year-old Matthew Henneck, and
his response of courage in the face of this stress was equally
inspiring. *Tribune* reporter Mike Peters again succinctly
recorded this emotion-stirring story.

> Matthew Henneck, the Greeley boy who
> fought a life-threatening illness for nearly half
> his life, died at his home early Tuesday.
>
> Matthew was 14 years old when he died and
> his mother, Mary, said he would have entered
> Greeley West High School today if he was
> strong enough.
>
> He planned his own funeral at the same time
> he planned his up-coming year in school.
>
> But his strength was failing and Matthew
> spent the past month in bed. "He knew he
> was going to die," Mary said this morning
> from the family home in west Greeley. "A
> week ago, we lost him twice, but he came
> back. He told us he had something to do,
> and he wanted to live another week."
>
> He made it through the week and spent the
> time saying good-bye to friends, his mother said.

A deeply religious family, the Hennecks
believe Matthew had a mission. "I think it
was to reach as many people as he could—and
he accomplished that," Mary said.

Once again a child had faced extreme stress with courage
that, astoundingly, uplifted and strengthened even his
parents! And again, his source of strength lay in the fact that
he shared the same "Secret" that sustained young Mark
Alexander.

In yet another situation filled with the stress of extreme
adversity, reported in the April 29, 1985 *Denver Post*, page 4-
A, a fifteen-year-old Rifle, Colorado, teenager struggled for her
life after a tragic rafting accident on the Colorado River. Three
months after Marcia Antes was trapped underwater, she
courageously fought for full rehabilitation, optimistically facing
her physical and mental impairments with steady courage.
Marcia Antes and her parents also knew "The Secret."

"We know God is in control," said Phil
Antes. "Whatever happens, we know that
God can work good out of it."

In each of the cases of extreme stress recorded on these
pages, the stress of adversity attacked a young person's well-
being in the form of personal tragedy. It is impossible, of
course, to predict which children will have to cope with the
stress of personal tragedy. A few will have to handle the stress
of a terminal or crippling illness. Some will face the stress of a
serious accident. They may have to cope with seeing a loved
one suffer death, disease, accident, financial problems,
addiction, emotional illness, separation, loneliness, or divorce.

Secular books and articles about helping children
manage stress devote whole chapters to different types of
adversity. While there is nothing wrong with some of the

suggestions of secular professionals, it should be noted that the real strength to manage the stress of tragedy comes through the development of inner strength—the kind of character shown by the children whose moments of victory over crisis have graced these pages.

This book does not treat each type of tragedy individually. Rather, the approach to managing tragedy of all kinds, whether it be the trauma of death, divorce, or disease, is found in "The Secret" which is taught in these Scriptures:

> Be anxious for nothing, but in everything by prayer and supplication with thanksgiving let your request be made known to God. And the peace of God, which surpasses all comprehension, shall guard your hearts and your minds in Christ Jesus. Finally, brethren, whatever is true, whatever is honorable, whatever is right, whatever is pure, whatever is lovely, whatever is of good repute, if there is any excellence and if anything worthy of praise, let your mind dwell on these things. (Philippians 4:6-8)

> Not that I speak from want; for I have learned to be content in whatever circumstances I am. I know how to get along with humble means, and I also know how to live in prosperity; in any and every circumstance I have learned the secret of being filled and going hungry, both of having abundance and suffering need. I can do all things through Him who strengthens me. (Philippians 4:11-13)

The Secret, summarized, is this: *God is totally in control of our lives; He is intimately aware of every detail of our sufferings, our hurts, our pains, and our heartaches, and He will give us grace and strength to face adversity when it comes.* As Christian parents, it is important that we give our children a reservoir of supernatural power to draw from when the fires of adversity threaten to consume their peace of mind. This reservoir can only be built and filled with God's Word. Some verses that should be included are:

Proverbs 3:5-6	Romans 5:3-8
Proverbs 3:25-32	Romans 8:28-29
Proverbs 15:1	Romans 8:31
Proverbs 29:26	Romans 8:37-39
Isaiah 41:10	I Corinthians 10:31
Matthew 6:31-34	Philippians 4:6-7,13
Matthew 10:28-33	II Timothy 1:7
Romans 3:21-24	II Timothy 2:1,13,15

Care should be taken to explain each verse fully to a child. Remember, the verses are powerful weapons for children *only* if children understand them and can repeat them in time of trouble!

WHAT WE MUST TEACH OUR CHILDREN

Since it is almost a certainty that our children will face the stress of extreme adversity in the form of life's tragedies either as children or, later, as adults with children of their own, we must teach them these facts:

1. *God is sovereign.* He is totally in control of our lives (Psalms 24:1; 31:14-15; 75:6-7; Ezekial 18:4; Jeremiah 29:11; Acts 17:24-26; I Timothy 6:15-16).

2. *God is our help.* He has promised to be with us through any adversity (Psalms 32:6-8; 34:4,19; 91:1-16; Isaiah 40:29-31; 43:2; II Corinthians 12:9-10; Hebrews 4:15-16).

3. *God is trustworthy.* All things work together for our spiritual good (Deuteronomy 32:4; Joshua 23:14; Psalm

40:10; 121:3-4; Romans 8:28-29; Philippians 1:19-21; Titus 1:2).

4. *God is all-knowing.* He is totally aware of our situation (I Samuel 2:3; I Chronicles 28:9; Psalm 33:13-15; Isaiah 45:4; Jonah 1-4; Matthew 10:28-31; Acts 2:22-24; I Thessalonians 3:1-7).

When we face stress, we do not have to fear what will happen (Romans 5:3-6, 8:28-29). The key is faith. Faith that we can claim for ourselves as well as our children. If we believe in God's faithfulness, we will communicate that to our children. It is a primary element in the bulwark we build to help protect our children from stress.

BRAINWASHING OUR CHILDREN

What I have been talking about is not mere head knowledge or simple lip service. What I am talking about is *total dedication* to shaping, structuring, and nurturing the hearts and minds of our children. It is the absolute, deadly serious, life-and-death instilling and inculcation of total commitment to Jesus Christ. We must try to brainwash our children in faith—so completely that their brains are washed clean of uncertainty, shaky self-reliance, fear, anxiety, worry, lack of confidence, and concern about their security.

Because secular and unspiritual values have so thoroughly insinuated themselves into child-rearing and child-education philosophies, many Christian parents recoil at the mere mention of the term "brainwashing." Nevertheless, brainwashing is precisely what the Scripture demands that we do, for what else is an education based upon these words:

> And these words which I command you
> today shall be in your heart; you shall teach
> them diligently to your children, and shall
> talk of them when you sit in your house,
> when you walk by the way, when you lie

down, and when you rise up. (Deuteronomy
6:6-7 NKJV)

The word "diligently" means
- without fail
- systematically
- with urgency
- seriously
- deliberately
- purposefully
- responsibly
- earnestly
- with deep attention
- with concentrated effort
- with total commitment
- with dedication

The whole concept of total education—total immersion,
inculcation, brainwashing—is expanded upon in the words
of Proverbs 22:6. In Deuteronomy 6:6, God admonishes us
to *teach*. In Proverbs 22:6, He commands us to *train*. Other
Scripture verses add to the importance in such passages as
Psalm 78:3-8; Isaiah 28:9, and Joel 1:3.

THE STRESS-TRIUMPHANT CHILD

Suppose you are convinced that the words of Deuteronomy 6:6 are to be obeyed with deep reverence: that you
will, indeed, make a commitment to talk about God's Word
when you are in your house, when you're outside, when
you're winding up the day, when you're starting off a day;
that is, *in every opportunity*. What will be the results of such
diligent effort? Will you build a stress-triumphant personality
in your child?

This is the answer provided in God's Word. If you teach
your children the Word positively and enthusiastically—teach
them to memorize Scripture, teach them about heroes and

heroines of faith, teach them to walk in God's way—the Word of God will do these things for children.

1. The Word gives the wisdom to choose salvation through Jesus Christ (II Timothy 3:15).

2. The Word provides protection (Psalm 119:11,105).

3. The Word furnishes insight, good judgment, wisdom, encouragement, and the ability to avoid evil by making good decisions (Psalm 19:7-11; Acts 20:32).

4. The Word instills confidence, security, recognition of wrong actions (Proverbs 14:26; Psalm 119:97-102,105-106; Proverbs 3:1-4; Hebrews 4:12).

5. The Word develops patterns of thinking that will be an "internal guidance system" for right choices and good actions (Proverbs 6:20-23; Matthew 22:29).

Children who are taught the Word of God will be more likely to withstand the stress of adversity, contemplate the possibility of tragedy or adversity without fear, and put into practice steps to manage the stress of calamity, if it does come.

Remember, it is *God Himself* who provides wisdom and ways to develop stress-triumphant personalities in our children. And that wisdom is available abundantly to every Christian parent who seeks it (James 1:5-7).

STRESS FROM OTHER FORMS OF ADVERSITY

Beside the stress encountered in tragedy, other types of adversity also lead to stress. We have already noted in chapter 5 the extreme results of inappropriate responses to the stress of peer pressure. There are also stress-related responses when children face challenges to their belief systems by authority figures or by other adults. I have spent countless hours listening to young students tearfully describe how they "don't know what to believe anymore," and declaring "what's the use of anything" as a result of having sophis-ticated professors or other students chop away at poorly-rooted value systems. At best, challenges to a young person's value system result in emotional upheaval. At worst, children can engage in destructive behaviors which are nothing more than inappropriate responses to stress. Worse than that, though, is that each of these inappropriate responses to stress is guaranteed to produce further stress:

1. Going along with the crowd and abandoning their own values.

2. Submitting to an autocratic, authoritarian leader or group.

3. Seeking peace or escape from guilt through mind-altering substances.

4. Rebelling openly with antisocial behaviors.

5. Experiencing emotional trauma via switching from one value system to another in rapid succession.

6. Withdrawing from social or academic contact in order to "protect and preserve" one's values.

Rare is the child who can stand alone against the stress of having his value system challenged, either directly—through explicit teaching or indoctrination at school—or indirectly—through the influence of the entertainment media, the values of the culture at large, or the behaviors of the academic/social/recreational groups with which he comes into contact. The impact of the unspiritual values of contemporary society is powerful, unrelenting, and destructive. There are young people who have come from Christian homes and who call themselves Christians, and yet have become calloused and inured to values diametrically opposed to those taught in the Bible. They not only tolerate them but adopt and promote them!

Our children face severe, extreme, and unrelenting stress through the assault of the world on their Christian value system. Their capitulation may be subtle; they may surrender in seemingly small ways. For example, research reported by the Associated Press concerning junior-high-school students revealed that:

> Junior high school girls who had excellent
> grades in elementary school apparently
> suppressed their skills in exchange for a better
> self-image and greater acceptance. . . . At this
> age, girls may be making compromises that
> are detrimental to their long term futures.
> (*The Denver Post*, March 1, 1986, p. A-3)

Other surveys reveal that:

- as early as fourth grade, 70% of girls say that they are "on a diet," probably in pursuit of a media-created "thin-is-in" image;
- in Los Angeles, California, at any time, at least twenty percent of high school students are under the influence of drugs while in school;
- despite the emergence of "sex clinics" in schools, teen pregnancies among unwed children continue to rise, and that 30% of the business of video rental stores in "family centered" communities is the rental of pornographic movies!

Research reported by Dr. Theodore Baehr in his book *Getting the Word Out* further confirms the pervasiveness and the damaging result of anti-Christian values upon children.

> . . . preschool children imitate the aggressive
> behavior they observe on television . . ." and
> ". . . research . . . show[s] . . . a connection
> between the viewing of televised violence and
> later aggressive behavior.[1]

Dr. Baehr cites additional research which demonstrates a relationship between the frequency of anti-social, carnally-motivated behaviors and the influence of television.

Children, from extremely young ages, through puberty, their teenage years, and young adulthood, face tremendous stress, both direct and indirect upon their basic belief systems. Incredibly, many Christian parents have followed the philosophy that children should be exposed to a variety of value systems and religions, and then "choose their own" belief systems, relegating saving faith in Jesus Christ to the level of choosing a confection from a vending machine. This "Freedom of Choice" is the Baal—the false god—of the last decades of the twentieth century.

The Apostle Paul warns Christians of these times. As you read—think of the stresses involved.

> But realize this, that in the last days difficult times will come. For men will be lovers of self, lovers of money, boastful, arrogant, revilers, disobedient to parents, ungrateful, unholy, unloving, irreconcilable, malicious gossips, without self-control, brutal, haters of good, treacherous, reckless, conceited, lovers of pleasure rather than lovers of God; holding to a form of godliness, although they have denied its power; and avoid such men as these. For among them are those who enter into households and captivate weak women weighed down with sins, led on by various impulses, always learning and never able to come to the knowledge of the truth.
> (II Timothy 3:1-7)

> For our struggle is not against flesh and blood, but against the rulers, against the powers, against the world forces of this darkness, against the spiritual forces of wickedness in the heavenly places. Therefore . . . that you may be able to resist . . . taking up the shield of faith with which you will be able to extinguish all the flaming missiles of

the evil one. (Ephesians 6:12-16)

Having worked with literally thousands of young people, I am convinced that there is only one way to prepare our children to cope with the stress of adversity. We must train them in the Word, live it before them, and equip them with unwavering confidence in the power of God.

One college freshman—a beautiful, talented, and popular young lady who was accepted, and respected, by her peer group made the following observation:

> My parents "brainwashed" me with the Bible.
> They literally indoctrinated me! But I'm glad
> they did. I know where I stand and feel a
> deep sense of confidence and peace. I have a
> Source to go to when I have problems. You
> can bet that someday I'm going to
> "brainwash" my own children in Jesus!

This young lady was the living embodiment of what God promises to us in the Scriptures. No attack on her value system will cause distress for her, even if a professor and a hundred classmates oppose her!

SCRIPTURAL STEPS FOR STRESS MANAGEMENT

To achieve the results listed above, we need to teach our children these things in order to equip them to overcome the stress of tragic adversity or challenges to their faith:

1. We must teach our children the specific Scriptures that declare, unequivocally and with brilliant clarity, that faith in Jesus Christ is the only way to salvation (John 14:6; Romans 3:23; 5:8; 10:9,10,13).

This is a tremendous stress reducer. It guards our children against the dangers of what sounds like the reasonableness of "tolerance" and "acceptance." They will not be forced to depend on immature logic or under-developed skills of reasoning to defend their faith against a rationalistically-oriented peer group or unbelieving adults such as teachers or employers.

2. We must teach our children the Scriptures which demand that we follow a standard of behavior diametrically opposed to standards the world accepts, condones, and even promotes! Our children should memorize these and similar Scriptures: Romans 12:1-2; Matthew 6:24; Colossians 3:12-17; Joshua 24:15.

Our children should have, on the tips of their tongues, Scripture verses that they can repeat to themselves and that they can share with others when their faith is under the stress of attack. They can avoid the stress of the consequences of inappropriate behaviors.

3. We must teach our children, by memory, Scripture texts from which they can draw strength when they are lonely, hurt, suffering, penniless, friendless, or otherwise assailed by difficulties.

I recall one particularly vivid example of the necessity of such reserves.

A young woman—a college junior—burst into my office several years ago. She was hardly recognizable; dark circles under her eyes stood in vivid contrast to her deathly pale complexion. "My friend," she blurted, sobbing uncontrollably, "she . . . she walked out of the dorm, went to an empty field, and she . . . she shot herself!"

Distress over a broken love relationship—a common experience for young people—resulted in the young woman's taking her own life. But other young people, faced with the same intensity of emotion caused by the same circumstances manage their stress with the Word of God and prayer. Your children can, too.

Questions for Parents

1. What major adversities has your child faced?

   How did he handle them?

2. What character traits does your child have which would enable her to face adversity?

3. What are you doing—or what have you done—as a parent to encourage character growth in your child?

4. What specific counsel on managing tragedy do you find in Philippians 4:6-8?

Questions for Children and Parents

1. Discuss together what character traits your child sees in himself that would help him face adversity.

2. Discuss with your child how her faith in God affects her ability to face tragedy.

3. List the four facts of "The Secret." Ask your child what they mean to him in practical, specific terms.

   a)

   b)

   c)

   d)

4. Discuss with your child what a value system is. Write out her definition of her value system.

1 Theodore, Baehr, Getting the Word Out (San Francisco: Harper and Row, Publishers, © 1986), p. 203.

CHAPTER SEVEN

What Else Can Parents Do to Help Their Children Manage Stress?

Putting Experience to Work for You

> An unwise man repeats his failures.
> A wise man learns from his failures.
> A wiser man learns from the failures of
> others.
> The wisest man learns from both the failures
> and the successes of others.

The adage above applies to man situations, but it is rarely applied by parents when it comes to helping our children. We do not often hear others admit their mistakes as parents. Nor do we try to analyze their successes, which, in many cases, are the result of accident rather than the end product of parental planning and implementation of specific steps.

This is a chapter about experience—the experience of bitter failure and of delicious success—in helping children manage stress. A collection of suggestions from parents follows. All of the suggestions do not fit into neat little categories, but they are suggestions which have worked for others and which can work for you.

Several causes of stress for children are presented, along with suggestions for either a) avoiding stress, b) limiting stress, or c) managing stress.

THE STRESS OF BOY/GIRL RELATIONSHIPS

It has been called "puppy love," and it is rarely taken seriously—except by the "puppies" for whom the stress of attraction to a member of the opposite sex is acute. This stress can cause poor school performance, discipline problems, inattentiveness, and a poor self-concept, especially if the "love" or "attraction" is not reciprocated by the object of a young person's affections. It can start in the early elementary grades. It can go beyond "puppy love" and become serious in the middle school years. And, it can present severe stress in the high-school and college years.

Several factors contribute to the stress of boy/girl relationships as well as peer pressure.

1. The stress to "look good."

While I do not advocate allowing children to buy whatever piece of attire happens to be in vogue, at times it might be desirable to help your child "look good," to be—in his or her own mind, at least—attractive to a "special someone." Even the most wise of children is not immune to being "smitten" with a member of the opposite sex.

There is no hard and fast criterion on how far to go in allowing children to "dress for success." But you can help your child avoid undue self-consciousness by being understanding of his or her need to feel acceptable to peers and teachers. The point here is to be sensitive to the need of your child to conform to some aspects of his environment. Even adults sense the importance of looking attractive, and that requires a degree of sensitivity to fashion—even if it must be limited to clean clothes, well-taken care of. No one chooses voluntarily to draw unfavorable attention to himself because of the peculiarity of his attire. Physical presentability does not necessarily mean conformity to anti-Christian values, or to "the world." It can mean having a message accepted or rejected, though.

2. The stress to date.

Extreme pressure for young people to date is not an uncommon experience. Parents sometimes push children into paired relationships before they are ready. Or, children feel frustrated because they are prevented by parents from dating, even though they're ready. The following thoughts may help you help your child to avoid the stress of the dating problem.

Ask yourself this: What is the result of serious "pairing"? The usual result is a commitment: marriage. Or engagement, which leads to marriage. Or "going steady," which leads to engagement. Or repeated dating, which leads to going steady. Or dating, one on one, which leads to repeated dating. In other words, dating in a one-on-one situation has an unstated, but implicit outcome: a serious commitment. If it does not have such a purpose, what is its reason? Logically, it can only be concluded that the purpose is to have fun with a desired member of the opposite sex; to get to know one another; to be near the object of one's affections.

Let's examine the above more carefully.

If the purpose of dating is not to initiate the process of finding a mate, there is no reason why boy/girl associations should not take place within a supervised *group* process. Pairing—the innocent exchange of special glances, words, and acceptable contact—is totally possible in the context of a supervised group, without the accompanying stress incurred through the exposure of immature children to relationships and commitments for which they are ready neither emotionally or logistically, or to situations in which sexual desire supersedes self-control.

One-on-one dating, if the progression outlined above is

accurate, is *totally inappropriate* for children under the age of about 16 or 17.

You can reduce the whole boy/girl dating stress by the simple expedient of knowing your children's friends and organizing "group dates" for them such as parties. This diminishes the stress on children to date; there will be no stress upon children who are not asked for a date; there will be no pressure on children who are afraid to ask for a date; there will be no stress on children who are not allowed to date; there will be no parent/child conflicts about hours, places, restrictions; and there will be no stress to find an appropriate response to sexual temptation if there is no opportunity to give in to temptation.

Step in. Take over. Restructure adolescent society in your child's community. Share the "group date" concept with school authorities and with other parents. Yes, it may cause you stress to do so. But remember chapter two? You are your child's first line of defense against stress. And the North American concept of "dating" in the eighties is a major source of childhood stress.

REDUCING STRESS BY HELPING CHILDREN PLAN

Scheduling, discipline, task-orientation, and routine all reduce stress. Having no regular routine, no self-discipline, and a hit-or-miss approach to finishing chores, doing school work, and having time for recreation are all stress producers. You can help your child reduce stress by being aware of the demands on his time, being reasonable in your demands, and by setting and enforcing a schedule. One successful family with two middle-school- and two high-school-aged children allowed their children to set their own bedtimes from the age of four on, as long as it was "within reason." They have the same approach to "hours" when their older children go out alone. There is a valuable opportunity to develop decision-making skills; there is a reduction of stress, and there is an overriding awareness of a sense of responsibility. This responsibility is instilled through early routines and high expectations of responsible behavior while the children are young. (See chapter 4 for a more complete discussion.)

Train your children to reduce their stress by helping them to plan each day. Discuss with them what their responsibilities are for each day. Take your time! Children have a marvelous capacity, at the eleventh hour, to "remember" that "they forgot" something major. A consistent investment of your time to teach your children to budget their time will be a lifelong stress reducer for both of you.

REDUCING STRESS BY AVOIDING "THE SHOWDOWN"

Few parents are able to be so perfect that they will never encounter "The Showdown"—open defiance or, even worse, irrational escape by a stressed out child. Many parents have experienced the trauma of having a child run away, or defiantly declare, "Okay, I'm leaving!" and then disappear for several hours, slamming a door in defiance or in tears. Equally numerous are the parents forced to deal with their child's blatant lies and the stress such lying causes.

Although the "experts" insist that such showdowns are unavoidable, the facts dictate otherwise. In fact, showdown scenes can be totally avoided by putting into practice one or more of the following actions.

1. Try to discern if the showdown is a cry for help. More about this later in the section on Listening, but there are times when open defiance should be ignored. Yes. Ignored. You may see your child's outburst as open defiance, but he may not even remotely perceive his behavior as inappropriate. He may be feeling ill. He may be overtired. He may be shedding tears of disappointment or frustration—but not with his eyes. Be sensitive to your child's pain. If his outburst comes from pain, be gentle and listen. Don't demand an apology. And don't force a showdown. He needs your help,

not your reprimand.

2. Another way to avoid a showdown is to state clearly your expectations—a factor discussed in chapter 4. If children have clear rules and consequences, there is absolutely no reason why an argument about consequences should ever occur. Where there has been an honest discussion of what Mom and Dad expect and of what son or daughter will have to suffer if expectations are not met, there can be no shouting matches later. There will be no regrettable "or else's" or excessive and intolerable consequences imposed in the heat of emotion. Hence, there can be no showdown.

3. A final and, perhaps, most effective method of avoiding a showdown and the severe stress it imposes upon both child and parent is a method adapted to school discipline, and one I teach to parents for application at home and to teachers for application at school. The method is discussed in my book, *Discipline That Can't Fail: Fundamentals for Parents* (chapter 8).

The method is quoted at length below, and after reading the introduction to the method in the first few paragraphs which follow, the reason why I have chosen to include this discussion in this book will be obvious.

> A few years ago, a particularly heart-rending tragedy rocked a small community in the West. Three young high schoolers, all outstanding athletes, students, and citizens, in a period of temporary stupidity, decided to steal some beer from a delivery truck which was parked behind a liquor store. Coincidentally, the police happened to be on a routine patrol of the area and they noticed the boys acting suspiciously around the truck. Each boy was found to have pilfered a six-pack of beer from the open truck, and the police placed them under arrest and took

them downtown to the police station. The boys' parents were called and two of the boys' parents came down to the station to take their sons home. The third boy, however, was allowed to go hone on his own, on the promise that he would return the next day with his parents, who could not be reached because they were out of town for the day. There was no hesitation on the part of the police in releasing the boy on his promise. His father was, after all, a prominent citizen in the community, and the boy was known in the community as an outstanding young man. In the minds of the police, perhaps, the purloining of some beer was merely a minor incident of prank-playing—a high school adventure which would be straightened out with a few words of admonishment from the parents.

Later that evening, the boy's mother and father returned home. They were puzzled by the fact that their son was not at home, but were confident that he would soon show up. After several hours and several phone calls to their son's friends, and after finding out about the pilfering incident, the father became anxious about his son's whereabouts. He called the police for help in locating him, assuming that perhaps he was postponing a confrontation with his father, whom he idolized, and that he was avoiding returning home until after his parents had gone to bed. It was not until dawn that the police located the boy. He was in a little-used vacant garage at the rear of his dad's lot. He had hung himself!

An investigation into the tragic suicide of the young man revealed that he could not face his parents after having stolen the six-pack of beer. They had had such high expectations of him and they had extolled his virtues so often, that he could not bear to disappoint them. He could not face the hurt which he was sure would be written on their faces. He had failed. So he hung himself.

The tragedy made a deep impression on me. I suffered for the boy's parents, who, like parents everywhere who love their children, would have forgiven their child any transgression, and who would never have voluntarily or knowingly imposed an unbearable expectation of perfection upon their child.

But how can we teach our children to adhere to the commandments of Christ, and yet teach them, at the same time, to accept and live with their inevitable inadequacies, shortcomings, and personal failures? How can we teach them self-acceptance, and even more importantly, that even though their parents, and God Himself, expect the absolute best of them, their parents will, by the forgiving grace of God, accept the worst of them when they fail—even miserably?

The first thing to teach children, to avert the kind of tragedy described, is to teach them that nobody is perfect, and to fill their hearts with the knowledge of how God handles the fact of our imperfection. Once again, the Scriptures come to our rescue as we attempt what seems like an impossible task—to teach our children that God demands that we be perfect but that, through the saving sacrifice of Jesus Christ, he accepts us when we are imperfect.

When I first read the newspaper account of the story of the prominent citizen's son with which this section began, I was horrified to think that a young man, a model of good behavior, would take his own life rather than accept the prospect of facing his disappointed parents. Clearly, his parents had done an extremely good job of impressing a high level of expectations on their son, but they had also created an intolerable burden for him to bear—the burden of perfection, with no room for failure. The son, it was pointed out by friends, had no fear of physical punishment or retribution from his father; nor did he have a fear of losing privileges. His only fear was the humiliation, shame, and guilt over what to him was a grievous and unforgivable offense against his parents.

My empathy for the anguish of this father and mother, who had without a doubt succeeded in instilling in their son the same level of expectation of quality behavior I hoped someday to instill in my own children, and who had suffered such horrible consequences as a result, posed an irresolvable dilemma. How could I instill a desire for excellence without imposing the unbearable burden of absolute perfection? How could I convey the idea that, although I might expect excellence, I also anticipated some failures? How could I teach my own children that, although I would admire and praise only their best, I would still love and respect them if they slipped to their worst.

The "Token"

The solution to the problem did not appear at once, as if by magic. Rather, it was the result of much prayer and thinking, but it has never failed in preventing a showdown. It works like this: On the rare occasions in which a child vastly exceeds a parent's highest expectations by behaving in a manner which is clearly extraordinary, the child is given a "token." The token is an uncommon privilege. It is the privilege of avoiding admonishment, criticism, scolding, physical chastening, or the loss of privileges when the child fails to live up to his parents' expectations. In short, the token can be used by a child any time he or she does not want to have to face his parents for doing wrong. The token is redeemable at any time. There are NO exceptions. This last fact is of vital importance, for the purpose of the approach is to allow a child the option of complete safety—in his mind—in admitting he did something wrong, without having the incident explicitly mentioned. He or she can admit that something very wrong has been done, without worrying about the humiliation of having the deed discussed or suffering any other parent-imposed consequences. the token system is absolutely foolproof in avoiding a showdown. It is much more acceptable for a child to avoid a confrontational situation by silently redeeming a token than it is for him to think he has to lie. It is far more tolerable to a child to admit guilt and to admit that he deserves the consequences by silently submitting a token than it is for him to face an outraged parent. A situation which could deteriorate into a highly-charged verbal or physical shoving match, or which could result in a slammed door signaling the impulsive independence of a runaway child instead becomes defused by the use of a token. And the end result is desirable: The child has acknowledged the wrong-doing and the fact that he or she needs correction. Self correction, though, rather than parental correction, is the result.

. . . Some additional considerations should be kept in mind when the token system is used:

First, a "token" is a *recognition* of an outstanding behavior, not a *reward* or *payment* for the behavior. Consequently, when the token is used by a child to avoid an undesirable confrontation, and when it is accepted by the parent, it is a *recognition* of the fact that we have our "bests," and our "worsts." It is not a payment to make up for the behavior.

Second, tokens should be used, as is the rod, sparingly. I, personally, have given only five tokens to my son [since we began this system]. They should be given only for behavior that is truly exceptional in terms of a child's hard work, maturity, responsibility, or Christian love.

Third, to be effective, tokens must be redeemable at any time, *with no exception*. Remember that the sole purpose of the procedure is to provide the child with an open door, no questions asked, out of a potentially humiliating, degrading, or threatening situation which he might go *to any lengths* to avoid, including lying, cheating, talking back, physical assault, running away, or suicide. If there are to be exceptions to the use of a token by a child, specify them in advance. But to be effective in providing complete safety in the child's mind, there should be no exceptions.

The token system, as indicated previously, has been one of the most invaluable assets imaginable in administering a program of discipline which is designed to be inspirational, constructive, and positive. As Christians, we are aware that, because of Jesus Christ, God in His grace does not always allow us to suffer the consequences of our failure to attain perfect obedience to Him. He provides, instead, the conditions in which "A just man falleth seven times and riseth up again," and we pray, with the Psalmist, that, "If Thou, Lord, shouldest mark iniquities, Lord, who shall stand?" As Christian parents, we can do no less than provide the same positive conditions for constructive growth, taking care to point out to our children that our patience with them and our love for them are a direct outgrowth of the love of Christ for us, and that our acceptance of them is not dependent upon their trading in a token. A Scripture which would be a most appropriate reference to share with children on this subject would be Romans 3:27-28 (TLB), which says:

Then what can we boast about doing, to earn our salvation? Nothing at all. Why? Because our acquittal is not based on our good deeds; it is based on what Christ has done and our faith in Him.

So it is that we are saved by faith in Christ and not by the good things we do.

In a showdown, even the "winner" gets hurt. Showdown prevention—stress avoidance—is the only approach that keeps everybody safe from the ravages of emotional confrontation.

REDUCING STRESS BY LISTENING

Statement: "Mom, I just can't talk to you!"
Translation: "Mom, I just can't listen to you!"

Statement: "Nobody understands me!" Variations include: "You wouldn't understand." "It's too complicated." "It's not important." "Oh, never mind!"
Translation: "*I* don't understand me!"

Statement: "Nobody cares a) what I think,
        b) about me,
        c) how I feel,
        d) all of the above."
Translation: "Please tell me that you value me and love me."

143

Statement:	"I don't want to talk about it!"
Translation:	"I'll eventually talk about it, but it'll take me a little time to know where to begin."
Statement:	"I don't think _____ is so bad. . . ."
Translation:	"Please help me admit this is bad, but in a way that I can handle."
Statement:	"You don't trust me."
Translation:	No literal translation possible. This statement can cover everything from "There are too many restrictions" to "I'm not sure of myself in this situation."

The statements above are commonly encountered. They illustrate one key way in which parents can help their children: by being good listeners. Several guidelines can help you really listen to your child.

1. *One thing at a time.* Don't listen and make your child compete with something else you're listening to or reading. Give him the security of your undivided attention. Verbal distractions to your eyes or your ears show that you are not listening.

2. *Try to restate what she says in another way.* If it is unclear, try to make it clear.

3. *Listen for the hidden message.* Don't restate the hidden message, but try to see if there is one, and gradually work into it.

4. *Be patient.* Count to fifteen before prompting or restating. Proverbs 29:20 says, "Do you see a man who is hasty in his words? There is more hope for a fool than for him." If you listen long enough, the source of your child's stress will come out. Luke 6:45 also states, "The good man out of the good treasure of his heart brings forth what is good . . . for his mouth speaks from that which fills his heart."

5. *Don't engage in an intense discussion when your child is overly tired or hungry.* What passes for anxiety is often dispelled by a timely snack!

6. *Discuss your own disappointments and successes.* One way to encourage communication is to share with your children your own needs, disappointments, and successes. If you have fears, discuss them, but always within the context of your confidence in the power of God to help you be an overcomer. One set of parents who openly shared—and received—confidences with their children received this supreme compliment from their teenagers. "Mom and Dad," they declared one night at supper, "you are our best friends!" The parents were good listeners.

7. *Reserve time to talk.* Talk that is the sharing of deep feeling will never take place unless opportunity is provided. For most people, that means dinner time. I strongly recommend that a regular time be scheduled to eat together and that the telephone, the television, and other "interrupters" be disconnected, allowing for a regular family Scripture reading and conversation.

8. *Respect others' privacy.* What makes us hide something? For fear it would be discovered, right? What makes us dissemble—engage in dishonesty or duplicity if someone bursts in on us, and we are in the midst of something we consider private? Because we're embarrassed, right? Each situation would cause acute stress. And then the embarrassment would cause further embarrassment, while both the person seeking privacy and the "intruder" attempted to recover from the surprise encounter.

The stress of trying to hide things, of deceiving, of being nervous about being discovered even in a legitimate, but private, pursuit, can be avoided. How? By respecting your child's privacy. You can do this by establishing a rule that everyone will knock on a closed door—whatever the room and whoever the occupant. Your child knocks on your door.

You knock on your child's door. More than stress reduction is won by this simple guideline. An important less is learned when privacy is respected. An important statement, embodying the lesson, is made: I respect your need for privacy. I respect your need to be trusted. I trust you, and I have confidence in you. The lesson transcends the child's room, and it transcends your home. It builds mutual, stress-reducing respect.

9. *Build a concept of dignity.* Another stress reducing rule at home should be applied to "secrets" and whispers. One family built respect for the dignity of each child by never allowing "secrets"—allowing a child to go to mom or dad and say something about a sibling. Of course, secrets that were fun, like birthday presents and surprises, were allowed. But secrets or whispers that took place in front of a sibling and that had no "fun" intent were not allowed. They were not allowed because they said, in effect, "You are excluded." "You can't hear this." "This may be damaging to you." The family had a rule. Behavior that built one another up was encouraged. Behavior that did not build dignity, respect, and love was discouraged.

Need anything be said, then, about fighting, name-calling or other types of conflict that some would tell parents to allow as a part of normal behavior? Name-calling, verbal aggression such as "shut up!", exclusionary secrets, or any other destructive behaviors have no place in a Christ-centered home. I have no hesitation in telling parents this: Insist that every person in your family treat other family members with dignity. The result will be children who command respect *outside* the home, and who will not submit to indignities which honor neither them nor the God who made them. Show no respect, and your children will neither give it nor expect it. Their internal stress will be lifelong and severe.

To summarize how a concept of dignity is built, these

guidelines are offered:

1. Respect privacy.
2. Respect personal possessions: some things are "family" things, others are "personal" things, including toys when children are toddlers.
3. No humor at the expense of others. If it hurts someone, ridicules, or uses sarcasm, it isn't funny.
4. No fighting or squabbling.
5. No "secrets" or "whispers" that exclude others. Putting some of these suggestions into practice will, no doubt, result in increased stress for you as a parent, since they require increased effort and responsibility. But these steps will result in decreased distress for you and your child. The results will be well worth your time and effort.

Questions for Parents

1. Your child may already have experienced "puppy love" or will in the future. How can you help him handle this type of stress?

2. What stresses does your child face to conform in terms of clothing?

   How can you help her to view these pressures realistically and make wise choices regarding them?

3. To what extent do you contribute to your child's feeling that he must "dress for success"?

4. Does your child feel a need to date or to be paired with a member of the opposite sex?

   What can you do in your attitudes or actions to relieve this pressure?

5. List the basic rules and consequences in your home.

Basic Rule   Consequences

6. What specific things can you do to build your child's self-respect and dignity?

Questions for Children and Parents

1. Discuss with your child the purpose and consequences of dating. Ask him what advantages and disadvantages he sees.

2. Ask if she is comfortable with a member of the opposite sex and what you can do to help. Role play specific situations together.

3. Ask what pressures your child feels from his friends and peers in terms of dress. Discuss how to make wise choices.

4. Work out with your child a mutually acceptable schedule. Be specific about tasks, consequences, and benefits.

5. Share with your child the list you made for Question 7 on the basic rules and consequences of your household.

6. Ask your child if she feels respected. Discuss what respect means and how it is achieved.

CHAPTER EIGHT

Taking the Easy Way Out

W**HAT AN ABSOLUTE JOY** parenthood would be if we could have children who:

1. Automatically turned to their parents for advice, rather than seeking counsel from peers or from other adults who may or may not share their values.

2. Could discuss any subject with their mother or father and who are confident and relaxed in doing so.

3. On their own, sought to grow spiritually by reading and sharing God's Word, by prayer, and by fellowship.

4. Recognized peer pressure and destructive peer or social values, and who are able, with God-given insight and strength, to withstand spiritually destructive values or pressures.

5. Approached the stress of adversity or of tragedy with a quiet and resolute faith in the power of a personal Savior to help them.

6. Treated others with respect, who apologized when they were wrong, and who were sensitive to the needs of others.

7. Stood up for what was right, who were willing to be rejected, ridiculed, or abused as a result of helping other children who were the victims of rejection.

8. Cared about the spiritual well-being of others and who were "not ashamed of the gospel of Christ."

9. Were motivated toward excellence in all pursuits by an inner motivation, rather than by external pressure.

10. Could be trusted by their parents to act prudently, with discretion and wisdom, even when they were unsupervised.

11. Embodied Psalm 127:3-5—

> Behold, children are a gift of the Lord; the
> fruit of the womb is a reward. Like arrows in
> the hand of a warrior, so are the children of
> one's youth. How blessed is the man whose
> quiver is full of them; they shall not be
> ashamed, when they speak with their enemies
> in the gate.

Many adults would shake their heads knowingly, cynically chuckle, and say something like, "dream on." But they are misinformed.

I have met such children, some of whom are now young adults with children of their own. Many of them have suffered severe stress, but they have not succumbed to distress. They are children whose parents took the *easy* way out. Let me explain.

In this book, as in many other books about children and stress, there are many specific suggestions for what to do to help your children avoid or reduce stress. But our ultimate objective is to help our children develop inner strength and personal wisdom. We have no guarantee that God will grant us a "tomorrow," or a "next year" to be there when our children need us. It is almost a certainty that some parent reading these words will have only a few days, weeks, months, or, at best, years left to live, to help his or her child manage and survive what Scripture calls "the fiery darts of the wicked." That parent, however, can take *The Easy Way Out*. In the final analysis, it is not a series of steps, techniques, "do's," or "don'ts" that helps our children to be victors rather than victims. It is the building of faith—the creating and nurturing of young men and women in Christ—that is the solution. And that is The Easy Way Out. It is embodied in the Lord God's words in Deuteronomy 6:6-8, and in Ephesians 6:11-17.

> And these words, which I am commanding you today, shall be on your heart; and you shall teach them diligently to your sons and shall talk of them when you sit in your house and when you walk by the way and when you lie down and when you rise up. And you shall bind them as a sign on your hand and they shall be as frontals on your forehead. (Deuteronomy 6:6-8)

> Put on the full armor of God, that you may be able to stand firm against the schemes of the devil. For our struggle is not against flesh and blood, but against the rulers, against the powers, against the world-forces of this darkness, against the spiritual forces of wickedness in the heavenly places. Therefore, take up the full armor of God, that you may be able to resist in the evil day, and having done everything, to stand firm. Stand firm therefore, having girded your loins with truth, and having put on the breastplate of righteousness, and having shod your feet with the preparation of the gospel of peace; in addition to all, taking up the shield of faith with which you will be able to extinguish all the flaming missiles of the evil one. And take the helmet of salvation, and the sword of the

Spirit, which is the word of God. (Ephesians 6:11-17)

Live each day with your children, from their infancy onward, in obedience to Deuteronomy 6:6-8. You will not be disappointed. The commandment is truly *The Easy Way Out*. God is the ultimate Expert on parenting. He understands the stresses we face in this world. When we obey God, the Bible says,

> Your wife shall be like a fruitful vine,
> Within your house,
> Your children like olive plants
> Around your table.
> Behold, for thus shall the man be blessed
> Who fears the Lord. (Psalm 128:3-4)

May God bless you with the confidence that can be yours in helping your children survive stress without suffering distress, and to grow, becoming "strong, increasing in wisdom . . ." with the grace of God upon them (Luke 2:40).

Questions for Parents

1. What goals do you have for your child in terms of character growth?

   What specific things can you do to accomplish these goals or enhance them?

2. Outline Deuteronomy 6:6-8 in terms of your home. How can you implement this command?

3. How can the "armor" of Ephesians 6:11-17 help your children manage stress?

4. Write The Easy Way Out in your own words.

5. List specific ways Psalm 128:3-4 is true or can be true in your home.

Questions for Children and Parents

1. Ask your child to outline Deuteronomy 6:6-8 in
   his own words. Compare his response with yours.

   Discuss The Easy Way with your child and how it
   applies in your family.

2. List each piece of the Christian's armor and how
   your child sees its necessity in her life.
   Clothed in truth—

   Breastplate of righteousness—

   Shod with preparation of the gospel of peace—

   Shield of faith—

   Helmet of salvation—

   Sword of the Spirit—

3. Discuss with your child how God "parents" us as
   His children.

Appendix

Aurora Public Schools
1085 Peoria Street
Aurora, Colorado 80011

SUGGESTED QUESTIONS FOR TEACHER INTERVIEW

1. Human Relations

   a. Rapport with Students

   1. How do you want your students to view you?

   2. When students say they want their teacher to be fair, what do they mean?

   3. What are some of the things you do to achieve rapport with students?

   4. What do you think is the most important contribution you can make to students?

   5. How would a child in your room know that you care about him?

6. Why do you think you can communicate with students at the grade level in which you plan to teach?

7. What would you do or how would you treat the student who refused to do the work you assigned?

8. How would you counsel a chronic truant? A failing student?

9. Do you think the image a teacher conveys to the students is important? Why?

2. Additional Questions Recommended by the Author

a. Suppose a child expressed a religious belief you felt was not valid, such as, in a science class a child says that Jonah, in the Bible, was swallowed by a whale and after three days emerged alive. How would you respond?

b. What would you do to help a child who is repeatedly ignored or otherwise left out by his classmates?

c. In which situations do you think it is okay to ridicule a child as a disciplinary measure? (Parents: The only appropriate response here is that ridicule is never permissible!)